# SPEED SECR

G000272889

**ROSS BENTLEY**

**MOTORBOOKS**
INTERNATIONAL

Motorbooks International titles are also available at discounts in bulk quantity for industrial or sales-promotional use. For details write to Special Sales Manager at Motorbooks International Wholesalers & Distributors, Galtier Plaza, Suite 200, 380 Jackson Street, St. Paul, MN 55101-3885 USA.

ISBN 0-7603-1510-8

**On the front cover:** Author Ross Bentley dives through Laguna Seca's famous Corkscrew turn. *Garry Cutter*

**On the back cover:** Bentley coaches Justin Pruskowski, 2002 Star Mazda Rookie of the Year, during a test of the Quantum Autosports Fran-Am 2000 car at Buttonwillow Raceway in California.

Edited by Peter Bodensteiner
Designed by Katie Sonmor

Printed in the United States of America

# Contents

# *Acknowledgments*

A great sense of relief comes over me every time I complete the illustrations and text for a book. "It's finished!" This is followed by anticipation of seeing the finished product intermixed with a sense of "I should have added this," and "I could have written that better." But, through it all, I think about the help so many people have given me during the entire process.

Much of what I present in this book I've learned from my fellow Speed Secrets coaches Danny Kok, Tony Riddle, Don Kitch, and Ronn Langford. Each has his own special strength in race-driver coaching, and I thank them for sharing their experiences and knowledge with me. What a team!

Of course, I happily continue to learn from my own driving experience. Big thanks, therefore, to the Doran-Lista and Essex Racing teams, for whom I have driven over the past few years. I have appreciated every moment I've spent behind the wheel of a race car, especially when working and learning from these two great teams, run by Kevin Doran and Michael Gue, respectively. Seeing firsthand how they operate has taught me a great deal about the business of motorsport. I wonder if they will ever know how much fun I have!

In the past few years, I have probably learned the most about racing from coaching drivers, especially when I can then go out and get behind the wheel and test it myself. While I've gained something from every driver, from the ones I've coached by telephone and e-mail to the ones I've worked with through every test session and race in a season, I do want to single out a few exceptionally talented drivers.

James Gue helped me learn what a world-class kart racer goes through in the transition from that sport to racing cars. Thanks James. Your talent behind the wheel should take you a long way.

I'm sure I have learned as much from coaching Joe and Justin Pruskowski as they have from me these past couple of years. As director of driver development for their Quantum Autosports team, I've been able to test and put in place every one of my strategies and techniques, not just in terms of driving, but within the entire team environment. These have been "dream seasons" for me from a driver-development point of view; I've been able to use my knowledge of race car engineering, team building, and of course driver development. Their results have been nothing short of exceptional, and they have been tremendously rewarding for me. Thank you Joe and Justin for giving me the opportunity and for your commitment to using my strategies. The time and effort you two have put into making it work is the reason for your success and the success of my coaching techniques.

I continue to learn from working with my Inner Speed Secrets co-presenter, Ronn Langford, and the participants in our seminars. My knowledge level is heightened each session, and it's both fun and fulfilling working with Ronn and each and every student. Thanks to all participants and a special thank you to Ronn.

This is my fourth book published by MBI Publishing. While each one has been satisfying and enjoyable, this one may be the best. Working with Peter Bodensteiner and everyone at MBI is a delight. Thank you.

To all of the racers and colleagues who provided feedback on the draft of this book, thank you. I always learn more when I hear how other drivers perceive what I'm presenting in my books.

And finally, thank you, once again, to my wife Robin and daughter Michelle for allowing and encouraging me to do what I love—racing—and for helping me learn so much more about life.

# Introduction

After I wrote *Speed Secrets,* and after Ronn Langford and I wrote *Inner Speed Secrets,* some people have actually suggested that I "figured it all out." Lots of letters, comments and e-mails from all over the world told me, because I was able to help them so much. But guess what? The more I appear to know, the more I realize how much I have to learn. This book is more of my journey toward "figuring it all out."

In the short time since writing those two books, a lot has happened. In racing, things do not stay stagnant for long! Both books have generated many questions, some of which I've even asked myself. I hope to answer them in this book.

Since writing those first two books I've raced a lot more and I've coached a ton more. I've talked to some very talented drivers, coaches, engineers, and other knowledgeable racing people. I've spent more time studying data acquisition and video of a number of drivers. Even in this very short time span, the cars and the sport in general have changed dramatically. Not a day goes by without learning something more about this sport.

Every time I think I've got a bit of a handle on what race driving is really all about, I realize I don't. As my wife said to me one day regarding parenting, "the more I learn, the less I know for sure." I suppose that is why I love doing what I do and why it seems that despite getting older (if I could only figure out how to stop that!), I still seem to be getting better as a driver, and definitely so as a coach.

I'm sure some people are thinking, Just what the world doesn't need, another book on how to drive a race car. After all, a book cannot drive a race car for you. But, what a book can do is help you develop some strategies that will enable you to improve your driving abilities. In fact, without strategies specific strategies it is doubtful you will improve at all. Just getting "seat time" is not an effective strategy, and yet, that is exactly what most drivers claim is between them and winning the championship.

I hear it all the time: All I need is a little more seat time, and then I'll be really fast. I just need a bit more time to develop the feel and skills to drive consistently at the limit. Sure, there is some truth in this statement. But, to simply "sit around" (in the driver's seat) and wait for the seat time to give you the feel and the skills is time wasted. Call me impatient, but I don't like to wait for things to happen. I like to make things happen, and that includes developing skills. I would rather use strategies to develop these skills in a big hurry.

My favorite quote of all time comes from Albert Einstein. He said, "A sure sign of insanity is doing the same thing over and over again and expecting something to change." How true! And yet, how many race drivers head onto a racetrack and do the same thing over and over again getting seat time, and expect something to change? They expect an improvement in lap time simply through more seat time. For most drivers, this is not enough. Without a strategy or plan to change something, nothing will change. This book's strategy is to provide you with some strategies for change and improvement.

I will use examples from real racing life as often as possible in this book. I'll pick on the styles and techniques of some of the world's great drivers (and some not so great) to demonstrate what works and what doesn't when it comes to driving race cars fast and winning races.

I should probably mention that in setting out to write this book, I did not really intend it for anyone who had never driven a race car before. That's what *Speed Secrets* was for—to teach the basics, to get started. My assumption is that you will have spent some time on a racetrack or autocross course at serious speed, that you have some knowledge of the basics, and some experience. Does this mean that you need to have years of experience before getting something out of this book? No. It may be just as useful for someone who has little to no experience and it will help build the foundation for quicker progress.

Even if you are a beginner, reading and using the information in this book may help you develop your basic skills without acquiring any bad habits. That will give you an edge on your competition whom often spends more time dealing with their bad habits than working on improving their abilities.

As an example, a funny thing has happened with a number of road racers I have coached throughout the years: they have become very, very good oval racers. Why? Without trying to sound as though I'm blowing my own horn, the reason was me. To be truthful, though, it could have been any good coach. Most drivers I coach have some experience on road courses, and little to none on ovals. So, I spend a great deal of time correcting bad road racing habits. The first time they ever drive an oval, I'm there to help them learn the basics, develop the right habits. They literally have no bad habits, and so they learn very quickly to be great oval racers. That's what this book may do for you: help you improve without developing bad habits along the way.

The main difference between this book and *Speed Secrets* is that my first book was mostly an instructional book; this is a coaching book. This book is meant to fine-tune what you already know, to improve your racing skills, and to help you progress. In fact, my main goal is to help you learn more in a shorter period of time. Left on your own, you will gain experience and improve your abilities. My hope is that this book will speed up that process and teach you in one season what could take you four or five on your own.

One other difference between this book and *Speed Secrets*, is that you may have to give this one a little more thought. Where *Speed Secrets* was pretty much surface-level information, this book requires digging a bit deeper. As you read through, take some time to really think about what I say. Most importantly, understand why I say it, or why you should do what I suggest.

As in my other two books, I offer Speed Secrets: key points, ideas, strategies and tips that will help you become a better race driver. Many of them may seem like common sense, but using them as reminders will trigger a better all-around performance. They can be thought of as quick summaries of critical concepts you need to understand and use. You will find a complete listing of these Speed Secrets in Appendix A.

If you have read *Speed Secrets* and *Inner Speed Secrets*, you will find some familiar passages in this book. I will repeat a few things, but for a very good reason: they are important enough to repeat. It may be that I have gained a better understanding of the topic myself, and perhaps I have come up with a better way of saying it, and an easier-to-understand explanation. Other times it is simply because I want to emphasize a critical point. So, if you think something is simply a repeat of what was covered in the other two books, think again. This may be where you need to dig deeper and develop a better understanding.

## How to Use This Book

Over the last few years, I've talked with a number of drivers who claim to have read and re-read my books. I hope that's because the information presented in them is being used over and over again, and not that it took them that long to understand what I said!

Actually, many drivers claim to carry their copies of my books in their driving-suit bags, referring to them throughout race weekends. I believe this is the best way of using this book, as well. I think it would be a good idea if you read through the entire book, and then re-read it one chapter at a time prior to each race in your season. That way you will have fresh information with which to focus your awareness, without overloading your mind.

If you decide to bring this book with you to each race weekend, I'd highly recommend reading through the two appendices before and/or after each session. The Speed Secrets and self-coaching questions in these appendices will help you become aware of areas you can improve. This alone may be enough to take you to, or secure your position at the front of the pack.

# Chapter 1

# The Complete Race Driver

It's long been an accepted fact in motorsport that a driver needs far more than just the ability to drive fast to make it to the top. Some say that it has always been this way to some extent, but most would agree that this is truer today than ever before. Today's complete race driver is a package made up of the ingredients shown in the illustration below.

This illustration shows a virtual job description for the complete race driver, a driver who is or will be a champion and a superstar. Some of these traits and skills are pretty self-explanatory, while others require a bit

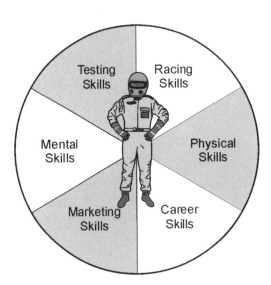

*A champion race driver today is made of the attributes shown here. However, they will rarely, if ever, be equal parts. Some ingredients are more important than others, depending on the type and level of racing and the specific situation or team in which you are involved.*

more of a detailed explanation and description. If I don't go into a relatively long explanation in this chapter of a trait or skill, it's because I cover it in greater detail elsewhere in this book or because it has already been discussed in my previous books.

Not all readers of this book will be interested in making a career as a race driver. Many drivers just want to have fun racing as a hobby. If this describes your approach to the sport, you may not think you can gain from some of the skills discussed in this chapter. My bet is, though, that with a better understanding of what it takes, this chapter will help you be more successful no matter what your level of racing participation.

## Racing Skills

**Speed:** Racing is all about speed—you need to be able to drive fast. Of course, that is a big part of what this book is all about.

**Qualifying:** Being fast and having good racecraft is not enough to make up for a poor qualifying position. You need to be able to turn in that one flying, magic, qualifying lap.

**Racecraft:** Speed and racecraft are not the same. Racecraft is all about passing, being passed, strategizing, and positioning your car to your benefit and no one else's. Some drivers are fast but don't race well—they don't have good racecraft—while others are the opposite. Obviously, becoming a real champion requires both.

**Adaptability:** If your car is not handling well during a race, you have three choices: give up, try to make the car do what it can't, or adapt your driving to best suit the way it is handling. Adapting is obviously the best choice. Having the knowledge and ability to adapt your driving to suit the car is one of the keys to becoming a real race driver. I will discuss this in detail in Chapter 11.

## Physical Skills

**Physical Build:** Let's face it, if you are 6 feet 6 or weigh well over 200 pounds, your options as a professional race driver are limited at best. Race car driving is not a big man's (or woman's) sport. If your DNA has led to you being on the large side, perhaps "OSB" (other sports beckon) is the best advice.

**Car Control Skills:** I have always believed that car control skills—the ability to control the car at the very limit—are more important than any other skill in terms of going fast. In other words, car control skills are even more important than the ability to determine the ideal line and drive on it. We'll delve into this deeply throughout the book.

**Speed Sensing:** This is the innate ability to sense the "right" speed. It is the ability to adjust and control the car on the entry to a corner, for example, to the same speed within 1 mile per hour, lap after lap. If you consider all the physical acts a race driver accomplishes, the ability to just "know" what speed to slow the car to—not 1 mile per hour too slow, or too fast—may be one of the most amazing.

**Traction Sensing:** This is the ability to sense whether the tires have another ounce of traction or not and then being able to keep the car at that limit all the way through each and every corner. Traction sensing is critical. It enables you to keep the tires at their optimum slip angle throughout the turns.

**Consistency:** It's one thing to drive the car at the limit through one corner, or even one lap. It's another to do it lap after lap for an entire race. Having said that, some drivers have a tough time consistently keeping the car at the limit all the way through even one corner. They drive at the limit through the entry or the exit phase, but not both. The goal, of course, is to drive the car consistently at the limit in each phase—entry, mid-corner and exit—of each and every corner for every lap.

**Strength/Endurance:** Driving a race car does require a certain amount of strength and stamina, more than some people could ever imagine. You should have the physical strength and stamina to drive a car with cornering and acceleration capabilities at least one or two levels higher than what you are driving today. You never know when the opportunity will arise to test for a ride in the "big time." Having a fitness level capable of handling a class above where you are today is also one way to guarantee you are fit enough for the level you are at now.

## Career Skills

**Business Skills:** At one time, most people felt that a driver would benefit from an engineering education because it would help him understand the nuances of tuning his car. While there is still some value in this, a business degree will take a driver a lot farther. Understanding the nuances of business is more critical to tuning one's career today.

**Team Building:** I call this the "Schumacher Factor." Is it mere coincidence that both Benetton and Ferrari became world champions during the time Michael Schumacher drove for them? No way. He made these teams world champions. He motivated the people around him to do whatever it took to give him the winning components. He elevated the personal performance of each and every member of these teams. The fact that many of the key personnel followed Michael from Benetton to Ferrari speaks volumes. You have to do the same for every single person around you, whether they are part of the race team, your family, sponsors, or supporters.

Whether you are a one-man team or part of a large professional race team, to be successful you must be able to get the very most out of everyone around you. And, it doesn't matter whether it's someone you have to contract with, your family, or the multitude of people on a pro team. To do that, you must understand how to motivate these people to go above and beyond what they will or can do without you.

## SPEED SECRET #1:
### No matter what level of racing you participate in, you are a team builder.

I've heard it said that the sign of a true champion or superstar in any activity is not in what he can achieve on his own; it is his ability to help everyone on his team, from the lowliest member on up, to rise up and perform beyond expectations. Some say that the Chicago Bulls won the championships they did because of Michael Jordan's abilities, and yes, his abilities were a factor. However, it was his inspiration and motivation of the rest of the team that was the real difference. He made every one of his teammates better players than they would have been without him.

That is what you need to do.

Now, I'm going to use a word to describe how you need to deal with the people around you that may sound unfair and negative, but it is not meant in that way. The word is manipulate. You must learn how to manipulate people in a positive way. The *Oxford American Dictionary* defines manipulate as "to handle, especially with skill," and that is what you need to do.

By manipulate, I mean getting people to do what you want them to do. I don't, however, mean this in a one-sided way; I don't mean for them simply to serve you and your objectives. I mean for you to get them to do what you want them to do and for them to perform at an all-new, higher level than ever before, to the extent that they are excited and happy about their performance.

As you know, there are many ways to say the same thing. For example, if you want people to do something for you, you can tell them to do it. Or, you can ask them to do it. Or, you can phrase it in such a way that they think of it as their own idea. Each of these methods will probably result in the job getting done, but only one of them will result in the person performing the task better than ever before. And, the method that works best for one person may not be the best method for another.

The key is for you to determine what is the right approach for each and every individual. You must discover how to inspire, motivate, and manipulate each person to rise up and perform beyond expectations. To do that you must begin to understand what makes the person tick: Are they a leader or a follower? Do they communicate and learn visually, auditorily, or kinesthetically? Do they like to come up with the ideas themselves, or would they prefer to follow someone else's ideas? When interpreting instructions, do they respond best to orders or will asking a few questions guide them in the direction you want them to go? And, when performing duties, do they want you to sit back and watch, or would they prefer that you join in?

There is no doubt that Michael Schumacher is one of the most talented race drivers to have ever lived. However, one of the reasons he is so successful is because of what he does outside of the cockpit. He gets more out of the team around him than any of his competitors and as much or more than any other driver in history.

"When you talk about drivers," says Frank Williams, "it's the single-minded approach that counts, and Michael is the master of that. He is truly a master in all the paths that you need to take at the same time while tackling the difficult job to arrive at the top. By that I mean he is the best at testing, the best at racing, the best at qualifying, and the best at getting the most out of his engineers, and tire company. The list is endless. He is always there working with them, and he pushes himself all of the time. He thinks only of winning. The previous man to do that was Ayrton Senna."

Four-time World Champion Alain Prost has this to say about Schumacher. "He's a perfect driver for F1 as it is today. I am very impressed by what he has done. His ability to drive a car is probably among the top five of all time; but what has really impressed me is he has created a situation at Ferrari that is unique. He maximizes his opportunities and he's always very motivated.

"I never managed to get a team to fashion itself around me for a long period. It is a big help to a driver, and your chances of success will be greater; but at McLaren, or Ferrari, I never had that. I look at Michael and Ferrari and I see him in a very friendly situation. He has a great relationship with the people around him, and most of them are there because of him. He understood the kind of ingredients that he needed to be successful, and it's pretty obvious that he has been helped a lot by [race director] Jean Todt and [technical director] Ross Brawn."

Notice that Prost suggests that Schumacher is probably one of the top five of all time; and yet Schumacher has won more Formula One Grand Prix races than anyone. That shows you just how important the race team really is. Schumacher himself admits this, saying, "It is impossible to be consistently successful without the right people around you. It took a while to put it together, but now I have a great team around me. The first few years were difficult, but overall, I have had a very happy time at Ferrari. The relationship I now have is very, very special; probably the best I have had in any team."

Schumacher has kept a strong core of key people around him. When he moved from the Benetton team to Ferrari, a number of key personnel moved with him. He is loyal to the people who have helped him win, and they are very loyal to him. That's very important in your efforts to build a strong team. However, you must always be on the lookout for someone better, such as a better engineer, mechanic, or crew member. That may sound disloyal and blunt, but it is a fact of life. Just as you must always strive to improve your abilities, you must always strive to improve your team with better people.

If you can't motivate your team to continue to improve their level of performance, it is less likely that you will achieve all of your racing career goals.

**Fan Appreciation:** While this trait will never make or break a driver's career, I mention it here because I do think a driver owes it to the sport to be respectful of the people who support his fun. Many drivers have become caught up in the ego-boosting glamour of being "superstars" and have forgotten who made them superstars. Other drivers never lose the appreciation for what they are doing and who played a role in making them what they are. It's not coincidence that these drivers often get the nod from smart team owners over drivers who do not have this appreciation and respect.

Speaking of appreciation, you need to have some level of appreciation for the history of the sport. While you do not need to be a motorsport historian, a general knowledge of who's who and who's done what can make a difference. There are people within the sport who do deserve extra respect for what they have accomplished. Be ignorant of that, and a contract may not materialize as you believe it should.

**Money:** Some may say that this is the single most important factor in today's state of motorsport. I don't necessarily agree. Yes, having the necessary financing is critical, but if you have many or all of the other factors, somehow the financing usually takes care of itself. Does that mean that you will not have to work at raising money if you have all the other factors? No. You had better be prepared to constantly work in this area, and never feel that it is "beneath you"—that with all your talent you should not have to worry about such things. If you want to make it, you have to continually keep your eye on the money.

**Networking:** Under the networking heading I include making and keeping contact with anyone and everyone who could ever possibly help your career. The drivers who are very good in this area have a way to politely stay in touch with people inside and outside the motorsport community. The term I like to use to describe this is "politely persistent." The overall objective is to have everyone think of you first whenever an opportunity arrives, and to continue to make new contacts with people who may have the ability to help you in some way, either financially, politically, or otherwise.

Many drivers believe that the only thing standing between them and the next World Championship is money. I usually disagree. The thing standing between most drivers and any championship is people. If you focus on surrounding yourself with the right people, the financial situation will look after itself. There are countless examples of how true this is. I realize now that this is what I did in my driving career, but not to the extent I needed to. Although I did spend a lot of time and energy on meeting and getting the right people to help me, I focused a bit too much on just finding the money.

### SPEED SECRET #2:
### Surround yourself with the right people and your career will look after itself.

## Marketing Skills
**Media Savvy:** Drivers such as Darrell Waltrip, Alex Zanardi, and Max Papis have been helped in their careers by their personalities, particularly

with the media. Something you need to understand, if you don't already, is that the media can help or hinder your career. Your personality and ability to use the media to your benefit will play a big role in your level of success.

**Public Relations:** Some drivers actually believe that playing the public relations game is beneath them, that they are so good that they shouldn't have to tell the world about themselves. Great! All the more opportunity for you, who had better learn how to generate positive public relations (P.R.) for yourself, your teams, and perhaps most important, your sponsors. The sooner you take some P.R. and media training and learn how to get your message across in interviews, speak in sound bites, and provide interesting quotes, the sooner you will become a complete race driver.

**Sponsorship**: Under sponsorship, I include the abilities to develop a marketing and promotional plan that benefits a company (and not just your own needs); develop the contacts with potential sponsor companies; how to "prospect" potential sponsors; how to sell a program; how to put in place an agreement or contract with a sponsor; and how to service a sponsor once you have one. Entire books have been written about this subject (*Sponsorship and the World of Motor Racing*, by Guy Edwards, being the best), and I provided a brief overview in *Speed Secrets*. Yes, this is one of the most critical areas of all in becoming a complete race driver.

**Sales:** When I talk about sales, I mean having the ability to sell. Sell what, you ask? Things like your services as a driver to teams; marketing programs to sponsors; team members on your ideas to improve the performance of the team; or generally selling whatever it takes to make you more successful. Some drivers seem to have a natural ability to sell, while others have to work on the skill. Either way, you need it.

### SPEED SECRET #3:
### *Marketing skills are every bit as important to your career as driving fast.*

## Mental Skills
**Focus/Concentration:** You need to have the ability to focus on the details as well as the big picture, and hold that focus for as long as needed on and off the track. The key is to be able to take in as much information

as necessary but not one ounce more. You need to acquire the necessary information without overloading your mind, and be able to maintain that information. This is a skill that can be developed and improved with strategic practice.

**Adaptable Behavioral Traits:** There are times when you need to be patient, other times impatient. There will be times when you need to be aggressive and dominant, and other times when it will be better to back off a little. There are times to be outgoing and easy to get along with, and other times you need to be self-centered and keep to yourself. There are times where the details count, and other times you need to forget the details and just "get on with it." The goal is to be like a chameleon, adapting perfectly to your surroundings and what the situation requires.

**Mastery:** Mastery has been defined as the elimination of unnecessary physical movements and mental processes. This certainly applies to the art of driving a race car. Mastering the art of race car driving means doing just enough and not a bit more. It is the very definition of what Jackie Stewart once referred to as "economy of movement."

It means turning the steering wheel enough to get the car to turn, but not a fraction of a degree more. It means braking hard enough to reach the tires' traction limit, but not any more. It means squeezing down on the throttle early and hard enough to achieve maximum acceleration, but not enough to exceed the tires' traction limit.

Mastery also means being aware of everything you need to be aware of at any particular time, but not overloading your brain by being aware of too much. It means being consciously aware of what you are doing, but not to the point of *trying* to drive at a conscious level. It means trusting your subconscious mental program to drive the car at the limit, but to still be consciously aware of what you are doing.

This is something you can practice every day of your life, whether you are driving a race car, a street car, or doing something altogether different. Practice giving the right amount of effort: not too much, not too little. Of course, it is important that your effort is aimed in the right direction. Putting more effort into the wrong thing will rarely give you the result you are looking for.

Mastery also means having the ability to adapt and improvise as you drive. You can always recognize a driver who is relatively new to racing. He is the one who is doing everything technically "right." Master race drivers do things both "by the book," and not by the book. There is no absolute right and wrong way of doing things. Masters do whatever it takes to get the job done, but in a way that is not discernable to the casual observer. It looks "right" because, in actuality, it is right. It is a master at work.

I discuss this more later, but the driver who can adapt, who can improvise the most and the best will win most often. Some drivers have only one way of driving a car or a particular corner. They are certainly not masters of the art. Masters can change the line they drive, change the balance of the car, change their technique, all at will, to suit the situation. If the track conditions change, if the car's handling has changed, if a competitor has taken the line, a master improvises with a barely perceptible, if any, change in speed.

Juan Montoya was a master of driving CART Champ cars. Changes in his car's handling, cold tires, traffic—no matter what, nothing seemed to affect his speed. He could adapt to practically anything. Nothing fazed him. He improvised as well or better than any driver ever. Montoya is a master.

A mistake many drivers make, especially inexperienced ones, is trying to drive the perfect line, to the detriment of their speed. Ironically, finding the last ounce or two of speed often comes from not worrying about driving the absolute perfect line. It comes from improvising on that supposedly perfect line and allowing the car to go where it needs or wants to go. It comes from experimentation, from thinking and driving "outside the box." It comes from driving creatively.

To a master, driving a race car is a creative, improvisational art. It's magic. Mastery of the art of race driving should be the ultimate goal of every driver.

A few years ago, I decided to learn how to juggle. It was something I had always wanted to do, and I had come to understand how beneficial juggling was to a person's brain integration and coordination. Once I had learned the basics, I would pick up three of just about anything I could get my hands on to practice. It seemed, though, that I got to a certain level of competence and stayed there. It wasn't until I started to experiment with tossing the balls higher, lower, and at different speeds and trajectories that I began to improve again. What I was doing was learning to improvise, learning to master the technique (although I think I will practice a bit more before I attempt to juggle flaming chainsaws!).

## SPEED SECRET #4:
### Adapt and improvise to become a master race driver.

Every now and then, go onto the track and experiment: try taking different lines, changing the balance of the car, braking earlier or later, turning the steering wheel slower or flicking the car into a corner. No, this isn't an excuse to be sloppy or for making mistakes. Think of it as a musician jamming or an artist just throwing paint at a canvas to see what happens. Learn what happens when you do something different. Discover what you can and cannot do, what works, and what doesn't.

**Decision Making:** Decisions on the race track are not like most decisions we make in our lives. There is not time to think for even a few seconds. Decisions behind the wheel of a race car need to be made in nanoseconds. That is why they need to be made at the subconscious level—they just need to happen without "thinking" about them. And they had better be right.

**Ability to Trigger Zone/Flow:** Great athletes in any sport have the ability to switch themselves on; to get into the zone or flow practically every time they perform. To be a great champion driver, you need to be able to trigger that kind of performance on a consistent basis.

**Ability and Desire to Learn Quickly:** The greatest race drivers of all time became great because they craved improvement. They learned early on how to learn, how to continue to improve, and they used those techniques throughout their lives. They have developed great learning strategies.

**Discipline:** One thing I've noticed through the years is that there seems to be a direct correlation between how successful a driver is and how he maintains his personal driving equipment. I have rarely seen a winning driver who wasn't almost fanatical about the care and attention to the organization, cleaning, and maintenance of his helmet, driving suit, and the rest of his equipment. His equipment is never just thrown all over the trailer or transporter. His suit is always clean, and he doesn't wear it while working on the race car. His helmet is clean, visors prepared.

It all comes down to discipline, and in this case, self-discipline. A driver will never be a consistent winner without it, both on or off the track. In fact, a driver's off-track discipline is an indicator or reflection of his on-track discipline. Without on-track discipline, a driver will not be successful. Undisciplined drivers crash a lot. They are not consistent. They do not give good feedback on what the car is doing. They are hard on the car, and therefore do not finish a lot. They are not good racers.

Discipline is what a driver needs to help him do what it takes to be a winner. A driver today cannot rely on his natural, born-with talent; many drivers have that and they work hard at developing that talent. And, they may have a better car or team, or they may have a bigger budget. To compete with that—no, to *beat* that—you will have to take your natural talent and work at getting every last ounce out of it and at developing it into even more talent. That takes a lot of self-discipline and a strong work ethic.

**Work Ethic:** Usually, a driver's work ethic is a result of one or more of three things. The first is experience; that is, the experience he has had in his life from the time he was born until today. It has much to do with how he was raised by his parents and whether he learned to work for things or not.

The second is motivation, and that sometimes has to do with the lack of success. If a driver is losing all the time, he may lose some motivation to work hard, thinking, what's the point?

The last thing is too much success. It is a problem I've witnessed far too often with talented, young drivers. In this case, it is when a little bit of success leads to an unwillingness to do what is necessary to stay at or near the top; to do what is necessary to continue to learn and improve. Some drivers have a little success, think their natural talent is the reason for it and that it will continue to carry them. Then they plateau and their career stalls.

The problem with success is that it often leads to contentment, a "don't mess with success," or "if it ain't broke, don't fix it" attitude. It happens so often: A driver has success early in his career, which he credits to all his natural talent, and then he doesn't continue to work at getting better. Meanwhile, another driver who did not show as much initial success works at improving until one day (soon) he is a champion, and the one with all the initial success is saying, "I kicked his butt back when. . . . "

Let's be realistic. There are fewer champions who had early success than those who had to work at bringing out their natural talent. In other words, many of the drivers who have initial success do not continue to work hard at getting better and they never realize their full potential. They never become the champions they could be.

Think about it. No matter how good you are, wouldn't you want to be better? Even Michael Schumacher works at getting better. If you want to reach the top, or stay at the top, you are going to have to work hard at it. For every moment that you are not working at some part of your development as a race driver, one or more of your competitors are.

**Motivation:** It has been said that nothing of great value was ever achieved without motivation. Well, that certainly applies to racing. If you are not motivated to do whatever it takes to make it to the top, you won't make it. This also applies to the ability to motivate the people around you who can help your career.

**Commitment:** I know of no driver who has ever become a champion who did not have to sacrifice a lot to get to where he is. That takes all the dedication and commitment one can muster up, and more.

Throughout my career, and particularly when I was racing Indy cars, I would speak to a person who would make a comment along the lines of, "I wish I could do what you do," or, "I've always wanted to drive race cars," or, "I would give anything to do what you do." At that point, I would usually nod my head and respond with something like, "Yes, I've been very lucky to be able to do what I do."

Of course, in the back of my mind I'm really thinking, "No, you don't really want to do what I do. You really wouldn't give anything to drive race cars." Because, if the person really did feel that way, they would be doing it. I also know that it wasn't luck that led me to making a living driving race cars.

My point is that if a person really wants to drive race cars, make a living racing cars, or become a World Champion, wishing it would happen will not make it happen. But if a person makes the commitment to do whatever it takes to get there, that person will succeed.

I often get people, usually males in their early twenties, asking me what they should do to make it to the top in racing. I'm sure they are hoping I will give them the secret code to finding the multimillion-dollar sponsor and the one single trick that will make them faster on the track than anyone else. So, when I ask them if they own a car, a stereo, or some other toy/luxury, and whether they have a girlfriend or wife, they are a bit confused. They are then disappointed in my response to their question when I say, "sell your car, your stereo, sell everything you own, and tell your girlfriend/wife to go away." That is definitely not what they want to hear.

I'm not saying that the only way a person is ever going to make it to the top in racing is to get rid everything he owns, including the love of his life. What I am saying, though, is that unless you are willing to do that, the odds of making it in racing are slim. If a person is not willing to sacrifice, and sacrifice a lot, there is a good chance they will never be World Champion.

I also hear a lot of young drivers complain that unless you are born into the "lucky sperm club"—meaning you come from a wealthy family—that you will never get a chance in racing. Ask Jimmy Vasser if that is true, or Buddy Rice, Bill Auberlen, or Tony Stewart. All these guys worked very hard at getting to where they are now, without a super-rich daddy paving the way.

If a person wants it bad enough, he will find a way to make it happen. Is it easier to make a career in racing with a lot of money behind you to begin with? Usually, but not always. I've actually seen wealthy kids get pigeon-holed into the "paying driver" role and never make it out even though they had more talent than some less-funded drivers.

I will repeat myself. If you really want it, and you are willing to work hard and make some sacrifices, you can make it as far in racing as your desire and your racing abilities will take you. Because, no matter how hard you work, how much or how little money you have, you still must have the ability to win races before someone is going to pay you to drive a race car.

**Ability to Use Mental Imagery:** Some people seem to have an easier, almost natural ability to visualize vividly. These are people like Michael Schumacher, Michael Jordan, Tiger Woods, and Wayne Gretzky. If you can't develop a strong mental image of what you want to achieve, in and out of the car, you will not make it. Fortunately, mental imagery is a learned ability, one that requires practice.

**Focus on Performance:** If you listen closely to what champions of any sport say, you begin to notice that they focus on their own performance rather than on the result they are after. This is one of the more difficult mental disciplines to develop, but it is a must. The more you focus on your own performance right now and how to improve it, the more likely you will get the results you are after.

**Focus on the Reason for Racing:** Take a moment and think about being in school. Recall two different classes, one that was a lot of fun, and one that wasn't. Which class was easiest to recall? Which do you remember the most from? Which did you learn the most from?

Far too many race drivers forget why they do what they do. They forget the fun and they take it way too seriously.

I'm not saying that you shouldn't take racing seriously. Of course you should. It is too risky to not take a serious look at what and how you are doing. But it is possible to lose sight of the real reason you are doing it: for the fun.

I know all too well from personal experience that when a driver is having fun and enjoying himself, he performs better. It is next to impossible to perform at your peak if you are not enjoying what you are doing. But you can't just tell yourself to have fun any more than you can tell yourself to be happy or sad. What you can do is focus on what it is that is fun about racing. You can spend less time focused on what is not going right, or could go better, and spend more time focusing on what is going right. You can focus on the act of driving, and on your performance, and less on the results (good or bad).

If you do these things and still don't feel as though you are having fun, my suggestion is that you look towards another sport or activity that you enjoy more. The so-called "glamour" of being a race driver is not worth the hard work and aggravation if you are not having fun as well.

### SPEED SECRET #5:
### Have fun!

**Intensity:** A driver's intensity level is a delicate thing. Too intense, and you will be trying too hard, you will be too aggressive, and your performance will suffer. Not intense enough, and you will lack the "go for it" attitude required to push for the last fractions of speed.

The problem is that there is no one perfect intensity level that suits each and every driver. You need to discover what that perfect level of intensity is for you, and then you need to program it. You need to be able to recall that intensity level at a snap. You need to be able to trigger it the second you fire the engine of your car. That takes programming, and the building of an anchor or trigger.

In *Inner Speed Secrets*, we went into the whole process of programming and building triggers. Practically every action you ever make in life is a result of a mental program—the software running your bio-computer (brain). For example, when you throw a ball, you don't think through each step of moving your arm and releasing the ball. No, you simply activate the "throw a ball" program in your brain.

Even emotions are programs. If someone cuts you off while driving down the highway, that triggers an emotional program, most often anger. With some intentional mental programming work, you can build a program that triggers the desired emotion. In this instance, instead of anger, someone cutting you off could trigger a relaxed, calm state, or even laughter.

That same process must be used to trigger your intensity level. Once you discover your ideal intensity, save it to the hard drive in your head. Don't forget what you name that file, and then each and every time you get behind the wheel of a race car, click on the "intensity level" icon and run the program.

**Patience:** Few may think of patience as being at the top of the list of attributes of successful race drivers. It is one of the great race driver's least recognized attributes. After all, most people would not think patience has anything to do with driving a race car. But knowing where to go fast and where not to (relatively speaking) cannot be over-emphasized.

Rick Mears was perhaps the greatest oval track Indy Car driver ever. Was he patient in the car? When the race or his car called for patience, Mears was the perfect picture of it. Then, when the race came down to the final laps and his car was dialed in, look out. Forget patience, he went to the front. Recall the pass he put on Michael Andretti to win the 1993 Indy 500! But had he not been patient up to that point, he never would have had the opportunity to make the pass and win his fourth Indy 500.

**Anticipation:** Why is it that some drivers always seem to miss the big crashes just in front of them, slipping through a hole in the melee that wasn't there even a tenth of a second ago, when other drivers, like magnets, are attracted to trouble? Some people would say it was luck, others great reflexes. I'm not sure it is either.

Part of it is the driver's ability to read the situation well ahead of time. By watching the lines and the attitudes (balance) of the cars in front, some drivers can predict when a car in front of them may crash well before it actually does. Of course, much of that comes from simply looking farther ahead.

Let me use an example to demonstrate. You are racing on an oval track, about to pass a car on the inside line. The car you are passing begins to drift up high. At that very instant, an experienced oval track racer may think to himself, "If he gets into the gray (the marbles, or loose bits of rubber and dirt and dust), he may get sideways and shoot back down on me." If you know that possibility exists, you can anticipate. In this case, you may ease up a little to give him a bit more room, or you may squeeze on the throttle to get past him enough so that he can't hit you if he does get loose, even if that means having to ease back off the throttle later in the corner.

**Belief System:** Another reason for being able to avoid trouble is a driver's belief system. If a driver honestly believes, deep down inside, that he has a special knack for avoiding trouble, odds are he will. The reverse is true as well. It is almost a self-fulfilling prophecy. Maybe even by fluke, a driver gets caught up in another car's crash. Then, a while later, it happens again. Now the driver begins to think, "why does this always happen to me?" He begins to believe that whenever and wherever there is a problem, he will find a way of getting involved in it.

Another driver may have a similar situation occur in front of him and be almost lucky to avoid it. He begins to think that maybe he is good at avoiding trouble. Then, another car crashes in front of him, and he avoids it. Now he knows he is good at missing other cars' problems. And because of that, he is.

A driver's belief system, what he believes about himself, plays a critical role in racing.

When I witness the amazing power of a person's belief system, I sometimes wonder whether a driver's inner force can actually overpower the very real limits of physics as it applies to a race car. Can a driver believe so strongly in his abilities that he can make his race car perform beyond what physics tells us is possible?

A perfect example of this was Ayrton Senna at the 1993 European GP at Donnington. If you were unfortunate enough to have missed it, here's what happened. This was one of those rare times when the McLaren he was driving was rather uncompetitive, and he had qualified fifth. It was raining very hard at the start of the race, but Senna literally drove around Michael Schumacher, Karl Wendlinger, Damon Hill, and Alain Prost (10 World Championships between these four drivers at press time)  on the outside of corners on the first lap. He went on to a victory that is part of Grand Prix racing folklore. Physics told me, and everyone else watching, that he couldn't do that, that he was driving beyond the limit. It was obvious that no one bothered to tell Senna about these laws. It was as if he just willed the car to do things that were otherwise impossible. He believed it could be done, so it could.

Can a driver's belief system overpower the laws of physics? I don't think so. However, do we know what all the real limits of physics are? When you start to look at what quantum physicists are studying today, you begin to understand just how little we really know. Already some things that Einstein "proved" are being shot down; just as some of the laws of physics Sir Isaac Newton proved hundreds of years earlier were.

So, maybe a driver's belief system cannot overpower the laws of physics, but it can overpower what we think are the laws of physics today. The one thing I do know for sure is this: The number one thing that limits a driver's performance is his beliefs about himself.

I want you to try something. Just close your eyes, relax, and breathe deeply and slowly. After relaxing for a few minutes, picture yourself at the start of a race, heading for the green flag on the pace lap. See, feel, and hear the cars around you. Stop reading this and go ahead and do it. Once you have done that for a couple of minutes or so, come back to reading this (no reading ahead now!)

Welcome back. When you first began to picture yourself on the track, where were you on the grid? First, third, or tenth? If you saw yourself in tenth, that is where you will be. Until you can see yourself in the lead, without forcing it, I doubt whether you will lead a race.

By using mental imagery as we talked about in *Inner Speed Secrets*, you can change your belief system. In fact, such imagery is a very powerful and effective way of doing that. And, until the day that you close your eyes and relax and immediately see yourself in first place, without forcing it, you'll need to keep using mental imagery to change your belief system.

Nigel Roebuck, in his "Fifth Column" in *Autosport* (June 8, 2000) made some observations about David Coulthard, in particular his fresh approach to driving during the 2000 season.

> In January, speaking of the season to come, he said he had concluded it was time to shed the 'nice guy' image, to put a low light on anything other than his focus on the world championship. Undoubtedly there was a feeling that he needed to deliver more consistently if he were to keep his McLaren drive beyond 2000, but I wondered at the wisdom of trying to reinvent himself.

In fact, I don't think he has. If anything, he seems to me more relaxed, more at peace with himself than at any time before—and this in spite of the awful events at Lyons airport just before the Spanish GP (walking away from a plane crash that killed the pilot and co-pilot).

To come through an experience of that kind has to change your perspective on life, to define very sharply what matters, and what does not. I could be wrong, but my impression is that DC has actually been less intense about his motor racing of late—and that his driving, his whole approach to the job, has benefited. There is a formidably insouciant quality about him now, which was never there before. Schumacher's words he should flick from his sleeve.

I believe what Roebuck, and others, observed in Coulthard was a change in Coulthard's belief system. This was particularly noticeable throughout the first half of the 2000 season, when his teammate, Mika Hakkinen, was slightly off form. A driver's beliefs in himself are developed through a variety of ways. Sometimes, as I see was the case with Coulthard, it was a combination of some deliberate work (mental programming) and a "happening" (Hakkinen's slightly reduced performance level). Often times, the happening is strictly a random, lucky occurrence. Other times, it is a happening made to happen. In fact, a happening made to happen is very common. In other words, did Coulthard's improvement contribute to Hakkinen's problems?

The other thing that Roebuck noticed and wrote about Coulthard was his relaxed demeanor. It is not coincidence that most athletes have that appearance when performing at their best. Rarely does anyone, let alone a race driver, perform at his best when "trying." Trying is a conscious act, not one that leads to maximum performance.

Tony Dodgins, in his "Prix Conceptions" column in *On Track* (June 8, 2000), quotes Frank Williams and Patrick Head talking about Ralf Schumacher:

> The Williams team likes tough drivers—men like Alan Jones and Nigel Mansell. Schumacher fits the bill perfectly. Ask Williams what he considers to be Ralf's main strengths, and the response is instant.
>
> "It's that very word—strength," Williams explains. "Great physical strength. And great mental strength too. Ralf's very tough in the head. Like

Jacques (Villeneuve). He fears no one. Without being conceited, he does-n't believe he's second to anyone. He automatically thinks he's the best in the world, but he doesn't carry himself like that. He's intelligent and usefully experienced as well now. And blindingly quick."

The strategies, the triggers, actions, centering, and integration exercises presented in this book and *Inner Speed Secrets* have a double-whammy effect in that they work in two ways. First, they physiologically and psychologically "switch you on." Second, if you believe they will help you perform better, they will. That is the power of the belief system.

Your mind, or should I say the use of your mind in a deliberate, productive manner, has the ability to shape reality. In other words, what you believe, and what you mentally "see," will become reality if you focus on it.

## SPEED SECRET #6:
### *If you believe you can't, you can't. If you believe you can, you can.*

### Testing Skills

**Technical Knowledge:** I said earlier that business knowledge is more important than technical or engineering knowledge, and that is true in the big picture. But the better your knowledge and understanding of race car dynamics and the mechanics of your car, the more likely you will succeed. You definitely need a basic understanding of what parameters affect the performance of your car and what you can do about them.

**Feedback/Communications:** Just having technical knowledge and understanding is not enough. At some point you will need to be able to communicate what the car is doing—how it is performing—to someone else. Champions have the ability to soak up every little detail as to what the car is doing, and then recall that information and communicate it to the crew when back in the pits.

**Sensitive to Changes:** Some drivers have a knack for feeling what the car is doing, while others seem to be along for the ride. They may be able to drive fast, but they can't feel what the car is doing, so they do not do much to improve and develop the car to make it better; they just drive it the way it is. Fortunately, this skill can be developed. Much of what this book is about will help you develop this all-important skill.

In many classes of racing, aerodynamics play a very important role in the performance of the car. Therefore, it is critical that you, as the driver, can differentiate between a handling problem that is caused by an aerodynamic imbalance and one that is related to the suspension setup. This is a question you need to ask yourself every time you relate a handling problem to your crew.

I've tried to describe the difference in feeling between aero and mechanical problems to drivers in the past. It is one of the most difficult feelings to describe, but I know it when I feel it. The best way I can describe it is that aero is a downward thing, and mechanical is a sideway thing. Obviously, it is somewhat speed-related as well. If your car understeers in slow corners, but not in fast corners, and vice versa, it is more likely (but isn't always) a mechanical problem. With that admittedly vague description, you need to work at being aware of when an aero change fixes a problem and when a mechanical change fixes it. If you do that, over time and with experience, you will learn to feel and identify the difference.

**Detail Oriented:** Driving a race car at the ragged edge in a race requires letting go of the details, letting go of worrying about what the car is doing and "how we are doing." But testing mode is all about focusing on the details, sensing every minute nuance of how the car is performing, and what can be done to improve it.

## Final Thoughts on The Complete Driver

The one constant in racing is that it is constantly changing. That means that this definition of the complete race driver today may not be totally valid in a year from now, let alone in five years. However, if you have two of the key components today—adaptability and a burning desire to learn—you will evolve as this definition evolves.

Every driver has strong and weak points. You can look at this in two ways. First, if you are weak in one area, that is the area you need to work on to improve, that is, if you truly want to succeed.

On the other hand, if you have a weakness in one area, you may be able to make up for it with strengths in other areas, to some extent. For example, if you are not so strong in marketing skills, you may be able to make up for it by being strong in all the other areas. If you are very strong in team building, you may be able to motivate a team member to take over some of your marketing duties.

Having said that, usually the driver who is the most complete package—the best overall compromise between all these areas—will be the most successful.

### SPEED SECRET #7:
### *The more complete a package you are, the more successful you will be.*

No, I'm not suggesting for one second that a driver does not need the ability to drive fast; that these other skills can make up for a lack of speed. Racing is all about speed, and no driver is going to make it far without this ability. I wouldn't have dedicated my life to learning how to drive quickly and how to pass on this knowledge if it didn't matter. However, in this day and age of motorsport, without combining all of the other factors with speed, it is unlikely the driver will go far.

# Chapter 2

# *Learning*

If asked what the main objective is when heading onto a racetrack, most drivers would respond, "To go faster," "To win," "To develop the car," or something similar. Obviously, these are all appropriate objectives. However, I believe there is a more important objective, one that will ultimately lead to achieving all other objectives. That objective is to learn. If you continue to learn, becoming a faster, better race driver comes naturally.

When you learn, you will continue to improve your performance. By improving your performance, you increase the chances of developing the car, going faster, and winning.

### The Learning Formula

Perhaps the most important thing that I have learned since writing *Speed Secrets* and *Inner Speed Secrets* is what I call the Learning Formula. It may be the single most valuable piece of information in this book—if you use it.

The Learning Formula is this: MI + A = G. MI represents mental image, A represents awareness, and G is your goal (what you are trying to learn). If you use the Learning Formula each and every time you are trying to improve upon something (which should be at least every time you head onto the track, if not every moment of every day), you will be amazed at your ability to learn and improve.

*Use The Learning Formula to continually improve: MI represents your mental image, A represents awareness, and G is your goal.*

A few years ago I was coaching a young driver during his first experience driving an oval track. One of the big challenges every driver goes through when driving an oval for the first time is allowing the car to run close to the walls at the exits of the corners. If you don't unwind the steering and let the car run close to the walls, at best you will be scrubbing speed, and at worst you will spin the car. So, over the course of a couple of hours of on-track practice, I continually reminded and told him over the radio to get closer to the wall exiting the turns.

None of my words did any good. He never got within four feet of the wall.

Then it dawned on me. I asked him where he needed the car to be while exiting Turn 4. He said, " About one foot from the wall." I asked him to get a clear mental image of what that would look like from the cockpit. Because it was a private test day, we took the opportunity to walk out onto the track and physically get a picture of what that would look like. He then spent about ten minutes relaxing, closing his eyes, and mentally "visualizing" his car exiting Turn 4 one foot from the wall, over and over again. He developed a Mental Image.

For years, I have personally used and taught other drivers to use visualization to learn and improve a variety of techniques. And it has worked. Using visualization greatly increased the ability and the speed at which learning took place. It is why athletes in every sport rely on the technique. But I also knew that this mental programming using visualization can take some time. I had begun to get impatient. I wanted him to drive the car close to the wall, *now*.

Around this time I began to truly understand the value of awareness in the learning process. So I decided to add this to the mix. I asked my driver to go back onto the track after developing his MI, and simply become aware—without trying to do anything else, including trying to drive near the wall. Each time he exited Turn 4, I asked him to radio to me with the distance his car was from the wall. Basically, I was forcing him to become aware, to add his A to the equation.

On his first lap, he came on the radio and said, "four feet." On the second lap he once again said, "four feet." Then, on the third lap he said, "two feet." And, on the fourth lap he came on the radio and said, "one foot." In four laps he had made the change we had been working on for 50 or 60 laps. In a matter of minutes he cured the problem that I had been telling him to fix for more than two hours. Simply by adding MI to A, he had reached his G—his goal. We never again had to work at allowing the car to run close to the wall.

As you can imagine, I jumped on this technique and have used it extensively in coaching ever since. I have also used it for my own driving. Whenever I want to make a change to my driving technique, I use visualization to develop a clear MI, and then I go onto the track and become aware. I build my A, mostly by asking myself questions.

These awareness-building questions are things like, "Can I carry more speed into the turn?" or "How assertive am I?" I might ask myself, "How far from the end of the curbing am I turning in?" or, "How far into the turn am I at full throttle?" When used along with the appropriate MI, these A-building questions help me achieve my goal quickly, efficiently, safely, and enjoyably.

### SPEED SECRET #8:
### MI + A = G.

I don't know of a faster way to learn anything than with the Learning Formula. Practice using it both on and off the track.

## Self-Coaching

I wish that every time you went onto a racetrack you had a qualified coach to work with you to continually improve your performance. I hope you wish for that as well. However, it is doubtful that will be the case, either due to financial constraints, or the fact that there are probably not enough qualified coaches in existence to cover every driver. Therefore, you need to learn to coach yourself.

Self-coaching is the technique of guiding yourself towards maximizing your performance and improving in everything you do.

Part of self-coaching is debriefing yourself. The primary objective of debriefing yourself is to increase your awareness, for without awareness, you will have a difficult time knowing what you should improve. You will not make any improvement, nor be aware of any progress.

One of the best ways I know of to increase your awareness level is to ask yourself questions and rate your performance and abilities in a variety of areas. For example, I like to use a 1 to 10 scale to rate my overall performance, smoothness, level of intensity, my limits, etc. To help facilitate this, I use a debrief form like the one on page 35.

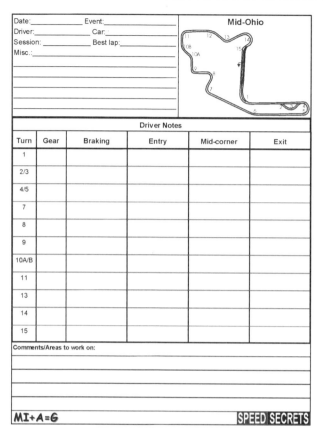

*Use this debrief form to coach yourself by raising your awareness level. After each on-track session, sit down and rate how close you drove the car to its limit in each section of the track.*

The idea of the debrief form is to rate how close you have the tires to their very limit. On a scale of 1 to 10, with 10 being the very ragged edge of the traction limit, rate each section of the track. Do this for the braking zone, the entry of the corner, the middle, and the exit of the corner.

### SPEED SECRET #9:
### *Increase your awareness by debriefing—even with yourself.*

Obviously, you can debrief yourself without a form like this, but I definitely believe that a driver who actually writes this information down gains more from this strategy. The physical act of writing something seems to increase your awareness level, demanding more accuracy. Plus, you will be more honest with yourself when you write the rating numbers down on paper.

Ronn Langford and I introduced the concept of using self-coaching questions in *Inner Speed Secrets*. In addition to using the debrief form, I recommend asking yourself a number of questions after each session. I've listed some example questions in Appendix B: those you should ask after each session and those to ask yourself before you even get to the track. If you answer them—even if you go through the process of digging deep in the attempt to answer them—you will coach yourself to a much higher level of performance behind the wheel of a race car. The overall objective of these questions is to help you become more aware of exactly what you are doing. If you are aware of what you are doing, and you know what you want to be doing, you will quickly and naturally make the necessary improvements.

## Learning Curve

Watching children learn just about anything is an educational experience in itself. One thing I've learned from close observation of my daughter is the steps a child takes in the learning process. Just when there seems to be no progress whatsoever . . . Bam! She masters it. It certainly is not a steady progression. No, the learning curve is more like learning steps.

Excuse me for a moment while I use my daughter as an example. When she was four years old, I decided that it was time she learned to ride her bicycle without training wheels. Notice I said, I decided. So, I went ahead and took off the training wheels, and then spent the next few hours trying to get her to learn how to keep her balance. It was certainly good exercise for me! The bottom line was, she was neither willing nor ready to take this next step. The training wheels went back on.

A couple of months later she came to me and asked to have the training wheels taken off again. *She* had decided it was time to learn to ride a two-wheeler. Within minutes, she had practically mastered it. Within thirty minutes, she was showing me how she could ride up and down steep hills while holding on to the handlebars with one hand!

There was no learning curve here—at least not when observed from the outside, or even consciously on her part. It appeared as though her learning curve was absolutely flat, then took a perfectly vertical step. In reality, even though neither she nor I were aware of what was going on, she was progressively learning.

And you know what is most interesting? All the race drivers I've observed or worked with closely follow this same pattern in their development.

The only drivers that do not seem to follow this pattern are the ones who get frustrated when they are on a plateau—the flat part of the curve. They get to that point where they don't feel they are getting any better, get upset or frustrated, and stay at that level or even get worse. The one piece of advice I can give about the learning process is that if you seem to be stuck at one level for some time, be patient. If you are using the strategies suggested here, you are about to make a big step up to the next level. You are about ready to take the training wheels off.

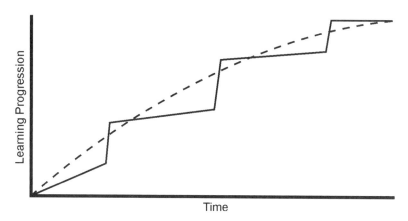

*The learning curve, as most people think of it, is shown by the dotted line. In reality, it is rarely a curve, and therefore should more accurately be called the learning steps.*

### SPEED SECRET #10:
### *If it seems you are not improving, you are about to.*

Over the past few years, a lot of people have talked about the importance of karting to the success of today's top drivers. Look at the grid—at the front of the grid, anyway—of almost any of the top forms of road racing today and you will see drivers who have grown up racing karts. Check out what they do between races, and you will most likely find them at a kart track of some type.

One question comes to mind to most casual observers: How does driving 30- or 40-horsepower karts relate to driving a 500- or 800-horsepower race car? The usual response is to point out the kart's power to weight ratio, the cornering grip, and just how fast things happen on a kart. All these things are supposed to help a driver keep in shape, mentally and physically. And they do. However, there is another area where driving karts of any type and speed can help a race car driver: *learning how to learn* how to go fast.

Every time you drive on a track, you are constantly trying to figure out how to drive quicker. At least you should be. If not, you are not a real race driver.

As you drive through a corner, whether in a 700-horsepower car or a five-horsepower rental kart, your mind should be sensing how the car/kart is reacting. You should be traction sensing—becoming aware (subconsciously) of whether the car/kart has any traction in reserve at any point throughout the corner that would allow you to go faster. You should be analyzing whether turning in earlier or later, or whether taking a shallower or larger radius through the turn will enable you to carry more speed. You should be experimenting and discovering whether a change in when you brake, how much you brake, when you begin accelerating, or how hard you accelerate means a quicker lap time.

In other words, you are constantly trying to learn how to go faster. And it doesn't really matter what you are driving to learn this. I drive a shifter kart to stay in shape and tuned up. I also drive rental karts on indoor tracks. I sometimes wonder which I learn the most from. Yes, the shifter kart relates more to my race car in terms of speed, but learning how to make a six-horsepower kart get around a slippery indoor track is just as challenging from a learning perspective. If learning how to find that last little "trick" to break the track record at the local rental kart track is your objective, you will become a better race car driver.

# Chapter 3

# Mental Programming

Much of what Ronn Langford and I wrote in *Inner Speed Secrets* was about "mental programming," specifically, how everything you do is a result of a program in your brain. An example is throwing a ball. At an early age, you observed someone throwing a ball; then, maybe one of your parents tossed a ball to you and asked you to throw it back. Rather crudely and without coordination, you managed to toss the ball—in some direction. At that point, a neural pathway formed in your brain, representing the physical act of throwing. You threw the ball again and the pathway became a little stronger; you threw it again and the pathway grew stronger yet again; and so on.

The first few times you threw the ball, you had to consciously think about how to do it. At some point, when your neural programming became strong enough, you no longer had to think about it—you just automatically, subconsciously, ran the mental program and threw the ball.

The same is true of the techniques required to drive a race car. At first, while you are learning or programming the technique, you are consciously thinking about how to do it. Then, with repetition, your brain forms neural pathways or programs, allowing you to head out on the track and simply execute the appropriate program at the appropriate time.

Think of it this way. Imagine taking a cup of water and pouring it on top of a big mound of dirt, letting the water run down the hill. The first time you do this, the water will try to follow the path of least resistance and begin to make a shallow pathway. This is much like the neural pathway in your brain after doing something for the first time—it's there, but not very well established. The second time you pour a cup of water on top of the hill, it may follow the same path, or it may find an easier, even more natural pathway. If it follows the same path, that pathway will become deeper and more ingrained, just like the neural pathway in your brain after doing something twice. If it takes another path, then it begins the path-building process all over again.

Now, imagine pouring that same cup of water on the top of the hill a few thousand times a year for more than twenty years. The pathway would be extremely well routed. It would almost be impossible for the water to follow any other pathway. This is what my own personal neural pathways were like for the mental program that operated my right foot when upshifting through the gears. After more than a quarter of a million repetitions of quickly lifting and then planting my foot back down on the throttle to make the upshift, I had to change that program when I first drove a race car with a "no lift shift" electronic engine management system. Instead of briefly easing off the throttle to make the shift—like I'd always done before—I had to keep my foot flat to the floor and just pull back on the sequential shift lever.

Needless to say, I found it difficult to not lift my foot at first; and for good reason, right? After all, with that amount of repetition, that strong a mental program, that deep a neural pathway, it was almost as natural a movement as breathing.

The good news is that for years that program was so well developed that I never had to give it even a fraction of a second of conscious thought. That left my conscious mind open to being used for more important things, like considering what a change in my cornering line might do, how a shock absorber adjustment might help the car's handling, or where my competitors were in relationship to me.

That is why it is so critical for the basic driving techniques to become habit, or mental programs—to allow your mind to concentrate on far more important things.

Now, the bad news. Any technique that has been programmed into your brain can be difficult to change, as I discovered when having to learn to upshift without lifting off the throttle. Do race cars change? Do track conditions change, requiring different techniques? Do all race cars react the same, and require the same driving technique? The answers to these questions are, of course, yes, yes, and no—meaning you have to be able to change or alter your mental programs quickly and efficiently.

More good news: Mental programming can be changed. How do you do that? Through the deliberate use of what most people refer to as visualization, but what is really mental imagery. Why the distinction between visualization and mental imagery? Because visualization, by the very definition of the word, uses only one sense—vision—in your imagined experience. Mental imagery, or what we referred to in *Inner Speed Secrets* as actualization, uses imagined visual, auditory, and kinesthetic sensory input. Please see *Inner Speed Secrets* for the details as to how to use mental imagery to change your programming.

## SPEED SECRET #11:
### Drive in your mind before driving on the track.

It is impossible to drive a race car quickly, at the limit, at the conscious level. In other words, you cannot consciously think through the act of driving—"start braking now, downshift from fifth to fourth, blipping the throttle at the right time, start turning the steering wheel and ease off the brakes at the same time . . ." Race cars are way too fast to be able do that.

Jacques Villeneuve had an interesting remark when asked to comment on 20-year-old Jenson Button's signing to the Williams-BMW F1 team for the 2000 season (*On Track*, February 17, 2000):

> F1 is 10 times more physical to start with, and then there's the speed. The first time you drive cars that quick, everything happens so fast. Your heartbeat goes up 20–30 beats per minute just because of it. It takes time to adjust. *You spend more time thinking about what to do rather than just doing it.* . . . You have to be able to adapt right away, but for it to become natural you need mileage. You can do quick laps, but *unless it's natural* you can't work properly on the setup and you can't do a whole race.

By "unless it's natural," Villeneuve is referring to driving at the subconscious level. And until the act of driving at the limit becomes subconscious, part of your conscious mind will be used for thinking about what you are doing, rather than being aware of more important things.

### Computer Simulation
Speaking of Jacques Villeneuve, he may have done more for the computer game/simulation industry than most people realize. You may have read that in his first season in Formula One he used computer games

extensively to help learn the tracks that were new to him. Prior to going to Spa for the first time—generally accepted as the most difficult Grand Prix track—he practiced by driving lap after lap on the computer. What happened when he got there for the race? With a limited number of practice laps, he qualified on the pole. At that moment, race drivers around the world ran out and bought more computer games!

I have to admit to not having spent much time with computer games, although I would like to more, especially with the latest stuff that's out there. In fact, these computer games, and more realistically, simulations, can be a very useful adjunct to mental imagery.

*Computer games and simulations are becoming more and more realistic, and therefore more useful training tools.*

I believe these simulations can be valuable in terms of helping a driver develop a virtual reality visualization, although there are a couple of limitations. First, of the three sensory inputs a race driver relies on (visual, auditory, and kinesthetic), simulations do a good job with two (visual and auditory) and a very limited, if any, job of the third (kinesthetic). Second, how much does driving an F1 car at Spa help a Formula Ford driver at Thunderhill? Mental rehearsal of driving one type of car on a specific track does not necessarily apply to another.

Having said that, there are things that a "sim driver" can practice that will help once on a real track. He can practice the ability to focus concentration for a period of time. He can also develop a fine sensitivity and control of the steering wheel. And finally, he can practice learning. As I said earlier, it doesn't matter whether you are driving a 900 horsepower Champ car, a 6 horsepower kart on an indoor track, or a computer simulation, the process of determining what works, what doesn't, what effect a change in technique has, or whether a change is necessary is one of the things that separates the great race drivers from the rest.

In *Inner Speed Secrets,* we talk about how a driver must be able to adapt his personality/behavioral traits to suit various situations, to control and trigger the ideal state of mind, and to make quick, appropriate decisions. If used correctly, a racing simulation can certainly help a driver mentally program and develop these abilities.

Overall, I think simulation is another tool that race drivers can and should use to develop and maximize their on-track performance. Just as only using physical practice on a racetrack, simply studying track maps, relying solely on mental imagery, or practicing only in go-karts will limit your ability to learn, only using simulations will not result in you becoming the next World Champion. But combined with all the other tools a race driver has today, simulations are very valuable.

### Expectations & Possibilities

Expectations can be a dangerous thing. Possibilities and potentialities can be marvelous things.

Expectations do not have any direction. It is like me saying, "I expect to be in New York City." That certainly doesn't get me to New York City, does it? No, there is no plan, strategy, or direction. If I say, "My goal is to get to New York City," it naturally leads me to developing a plan to get there.

If you expect a particular result and it does not occur, you become frustrated or disappointed. Neither feeling helps get you any closer to the result you were looking for. If you focus on your goals, such as performing at your very best, you then have a direction to follow, one that will more likely lead to the result you were looking for.

Expectations can also be limitations. Going into qualifying, for example, you think that if you turn a 1:20.5, that will put you on the front row. You head onto the track and do a 1:20.8, a 1:20.6, and then a 1:20.5. What are the odds of you going much quicker? Not good. After all, you matched your expectations. Consciously, you may not be satisfied with the time, but if you put a time into your subconscious, your mind will do what it takes to match it and not go beyond it. But, what if the track conditions changed for the better? Some tracks change significantly throughout a race weekend, becoming faster with each session. So, perhaps a 1:20.5 would have put you on the front row based on a previous session, but only put you on the fourth or fifth row in qualifying.

Karl Wendlinger, who was severely hurt driving a Sauber F1 car at the 1994 Monaco Grand Prix, provides a perfect example of this in Christopher Hilton's book, *Inside the Mind of the Grand Prix Driver*. In this case, he is referring to when he went back to testing for the Sauber team in 1995, having been away from the cockpit for almost a year.

> Because I'd only done a little driving I had time to prepare my body, to do training. I did a lot of concentration exercises. Then I arrived at Mugello. It was a two-and-a-half day test and, the evening before, I thought "OK, one minute 30.4 would be a good time." I concentrated, I closed my eyes and as I crossed the line into the lap I started my stopwatch. I did a whole lap in my brain and looked. The stopwatch said 1:30.4. The next day on the track I did 1:30.4.
>
> Then I said to myself, "it was too easy, tomorrow you have to do 1:29.3." The best lap that Heinz-Harald (Frentzen, Wendlinger's teammate) did in Mugello all year was 1:29.0 and because I had done so little driving I thought 1:29.3 was competitive. I sat in the hotel again, closed my eyes and started the watch. I "drove" the lap and looked. 1:29.3. Next day I did 1:29.3. You know the best thing was—and this fascinates me about what you can do with your brain—I only did the 1:29.3 *because* I made a mistake and lost three-tenths. If I hadn't made that mistake I would have done 1:29.0—but the evening before I had fixed in my brain 1:29.3 and not zero, and that's what happened. If I had fixed 1:29.0 maybe I wouldn't have made the mistake and I'd done the time easily.

Like I said, expectations are limitations, and you rarely exceed your expectations. Wendlinger proved that, along with the power of mental imagery. Expectations program results into your mind, and your mind is very efficient at running those programs; sometimes too efficient! In Wendlinger's case it sounds as if had he expected to turn a 1:29.0, he would not have made the error that ultimately cost him three-tenths of a second. That's the (negative) power of expectations at work.

## SPEED SECRET #12:
### Delete your expectations. Focus on your possibilities.

### Thoughts

Behind the wheel of your race car, have you ever thought to yourself, "That was a dumb move to make," or, "Why did I turn in so early for that corner?" Did any of those thoughts do you any good? I doubt it. In fact, I bet they did more harm than good. If you are going to have some thoughts while driving (and there is no doubt you will, at least I hope so!), make them non-judgmental thoughts.

Is there any danger in thinking about the past? There certainly can be. The nanosecond that you focus any amount of your attention on what has happened in the past is attention that is not being given to what is happening right now.

Can you do anything about what has happened in the past? Absolutely not. If you make a mistake going through Turn 2, does thinking about that while heading into Turn 3 help or hinder? Hinder, for sure. Does getting upset about how a competitor shut the door on you entering Turn 5 help? No. Like I said, the second you make an error, forget it. What you did, or what another driver did, is not important now.

Can you do anything about what is going to happen in the future? Yes. How? By what you are doing right now. When you focus your attention on the present, you increase your chances of performing at the level that will result in the goals you have set.

Having no thoughts at all is far more desirable than a mind full of thoughts. In the practice of Zen, they encourage an empty or beginner's mind. A mind full of thoughts is one that will not react instantaneously and naturally.

In his book, *Zen Mind, Beginner's Mind,* Suzuki Roshi writes, "If your mind is empty, it is always ready for anything; it is open to everything. In the beginner's mind there are many possibilities; in the expert's mind there are few."

The same thing applies to the use of mental imagery, or visualization. In your mental imagery, you want to actualize yourself as being open and ready for anything. Many drivers have asked me how they can visualize the start of a race and predict every possible scenario that could happen. "You can't," is my response. The same with trying to mentally prepare, using visualization, to drive a car you have never driven. How can you visualize something when you have no idea of what it could possibly look like?

Instead, you need to use a kind of open-ended mental imagery, one that sees you as ready for anything. For example, mentally see yourself at the start of a race: If you can't go to the inside, you go outside and make a pass. If you don't get a jump on the field, you make up for it in the second half of the first lap. It's not that you imagine every possible scenario, but that you are ready and make the right moves no matter what happens.

Michael Jordan, one of the greatest athletes of all time, prepares for high-pressure situations by recalling images of past successes. As former Chicago Bulls coach Phil Jackson explained in his book, *Sacred Hoops*: Jordan doesn't believe in trying to visualize the shot in specific detail. "I know what I want the outcome to be," he says, "but I don't try to see myself doing it beforehand. In 1982, I knew I wanted to make that shot (the last-second shot he used to take his University of North Carolina team to the NCAA Championship). I didn't know where I was going to shoot it or what kind of shot I was going to take. I just believed I could do it, and I did."

That's open-ended imagery. That's having an empty mind, a beginner's mind, one without expectations.

# Chapter 4

# Sensory Input

This entire chapter can practically be summed up in one statement:

### SPEED SECRET #13:
**The greater the quantity and the higher the quality of sensory information going into your brain, the better the quality of the output and the better you will drive.**

Think of it this way: Every little piece of information entering your brain from your senses (primarily vision, feel, and hearing, when it comes to race car driving), results in a decision or physical movement. And just like having more information about the financial performance of a company can help you make a better investment decision, the more information you have about the position of the car in a corner, where other cars are around you, the amount of traction the tires have, the precise speed the car is traveling, the g-forces and vibrations, and the sounds from the engine and tires, the better your decisions and physical actions will be.

Most people would agree that hand-eye coordination is a very important part of driving a race car, but few can give you a clue as to how to improve it. Basically, here is what hand-eye coordination is: Information is fed to your brain through your eyes, where it is processed, and then your hand (or any other part of your body) is instructed to perform the appropriate action. From this simple explanation, it is easy to see why any improvement in the quantity or quality of the information going from your eyes to your brain should result in a more "coordinated" action.

In reality, we also rely on hand-ear coordination, where information from your hearing is processed and the appropriate action is then performed by your body; as well as what could be called hand-hand coordination— kinesthetic or feel information providing the input to the brain.

Imagine trying to drive a race car along an ideal cornering line if your vision was restricted 90 percent. Or, if your body was completely isolated from the car so that you could not feel any of the vibrations, g-forces, or chassis roll or pitch. Or, if you were deaf, you could not hear any sound whatsoever from the car. Would that affect your ability to drive the car at its limit? Absolutely!

## Visual Input

Have you ever wondered whether what you see is what other people see? Have you wondered whether what you see, or perceive to be the color red for example, is the same as what other people see or perceive as red?

Have you ever wondered whether other drivers see as much or more than you do? Why is it that some drivers seem to be all-seeing, all-aware, all-knowing of everything going on around them, when other drivers seem to have blinders on?

It is a fact that what you see is primarily what your brain constructs. In other words, your eyes send to your brain a small amount of data, where it is turned into a lot of useful information. Most people think it is your eyes that provide you with what you see, where in reality it is more your brain. Vision researchers have proved this point. And that is why some people with 20-20 vision "see" more than others with 20-20 vision. Some older drivers whose eyesight may not be as good as younger drivers', for example, see and are aware of more.

Some drivers see a tiny flash of something in their mirrors and know exactly what it is. For others, that same amount of data from the eyes results in little to no visual construction in the mind; no information is assimilated. That, of course, is why some drivers seem to be able to stay out of trouble, whereas others seem to be attracted to it. It's just that these drivers are not able to make any useful sense out of a miniscule amount of data being sent to the brain by the eyes.

Think of a driver who has a reputation for making a lot of bad decisions and crashing a lot. To most observers, it is simply a shame that he makes so many mistakes, since he is so fast, so talented otherwise. They write him off as a serious championship contender. What's truly a shame is that nothing is done to help this driver improve. And the "cure" is often just a matter of finding the real cause of the problem.

For a driver who makes a lot of mistakes, the root cause of the problem is often a lack of quality sensory input, especially visual input. For instance, where most drivers entering a corner in a pack of cars may recognize that there is not enough room to make a pass, our "crasher" may see it as an opening. The reason is that for a fraction of a second, he is not seeing the whole picture. For a variety of reasons, his visual input is restricted. As you know, it would only take a very small piece of the puzzle to be missing for an error to occur at racing speeds.

When you think about it with this in mind, it is very understandable why some drivers make more mistakes than others, why they seem to be attracted to problems, and why they seem to make more than their fair share of bad decisions. I have observed race drivers doing Lazy 8's and Focus Stretch exercises in our Inner Speed Secrets Seminars who have 20-20 vision. Their vision may be "perfect," but I can see that their visual input is restricted by at least 30 percent.

Fortunately, visual processing is something that can be developed. How? First, by using the exercises and strategies presented in *Inner Speed Secrets,* such as the above-mentioned Focus Stretches and Lazy 8's. The improvement I've witnessed in drivers who use these exercises on a regular basis is nothing short of amazing. And second, through experiencing a short period of sensory deprivation, which can lead to an increase in sensitivity.

Consider blind people for a moment. Despite their lack of vision, their other senses (touch, hearing, taste, smell) are usually more sensitive than among people with sight. Why is that? Because they have been forced to more keenly develop the senses they have.

By restricting some of your senses for a short period of time, you are forced to develop your other senses. Of course, it is not something you consciously set about doing. It is something your mind automatically does on its own. I have, at times, joked about going onto the racetrack blindfolded and how that would improve your other senses—if you survived!

The same type of thing can be used to develop the visual construction process. If you restrict the amount of information your eyes can send to your brain, but ask your brain for just as much information output, it is up to your brain to make up the difference. In other words, send your brain a little bit of data and expect your brain to output a lot of information. Now, going on to a racetrack with your vision even slightly restricted is dangerous. But what if you practiced taking the same amount of data from your eyes as you usually do but asked your brain to output more information for that little data? What you are doing, in fact, is practicing being more aware, practicing using your brain's vision construction abilities, practicing being sensitive to visual data.

It is, in fact, something you can and should practice, and not only on the racetrack. It is something you should definitely practice while driving on the street, and also in all other activities in your life. For example, while driving down the highway and using your vision as you normally do, ask your brain for as much information as possible. Ask it to be aware of everything along the side of the roadway. Make note of the ground, the grass, and the trees in great detail as you pass it by. But don't just note that they are there. Also note the colors, the type and amount of leaves on the trees, the condition of the bark, whether the ground is made up of mostly dirt or of rocks, etc., and the speed at which they pass by.

When doing this, though, don't look directly at the ground, grass and trees. Look down the road like you normally would, but allow your brain to take in more information (actually, construct more information from the data your eyes are supplying to it). Ask your brain to provide more information. There is a physical limit to how much your eyes can take in. It is practically limitless what your brain can do with that information.

What you are doing is practicing becoming more aware of everything around you, using the same amount of visual data supplied by your eyes. Practicing this in your everyday world will greatly enhance your performance on the racetrack.

While driving in traffic on the street, practice being aware of every car, truck, pedestrian, and anything else. The more you practice this, the more aware you will be of other cars around you on the track—without having to put much, if any, concentration on it. The less focus and concentration you put into noticing where your competitors are, the more you have to put into more important things like track conditions, reference points, and speed and traction sensing.

### SPEED SECRET #14:
### Practice—everyday—being aware.

One of the more difficult visual challenges you face, especially on street circuits, is seeing around corners. Often, on road circuits—and, with the cement walls lining the track, almost always on street circuits—your view through the turns is restricted. What you need to do is see *around* the corner.

A few years ago, when Al Unser Jr. was at the top of his game on street circuits, I (and a few others) noticed how his head was turned and cocked to the side on the approach to a corner. It was as if he was trying to stretch his neck to peek around the cement wall on the inside of the turn. I wasn't sure if this was something Unser did on purpose—or whether he did it at all—but it sure looked like it. Now, I think it was something he did without realizing while trying to stretch *his vision*, not his head or neck, around the corners.

I wonder if this is one of the reasons Unser was so dominant on street circuits for so many years.

If you consciously try to stretch your vision—try looking as far around the corner as possible, even if it means using your imagination—over and over again when practicing, eventually it will become a habit, or a mental program. Then, it will be something that you do without any conscious thought—like Al Jr. did. It is as if you are building a mental picture to fill in the holes in the visual picture.

## Kinesthetic Input

Touch and auditory input are similar to visual input in that most of the information is constructed in your brain. If you were to practice feeling things with your hands over and over, do they become more sensitive? Yes and no. Actually, your hands themselves do not become more sensitive, but your brain becomes better at constructing the feelings from the same amount of data sent to it. So, in the end, they become more sensitive because your brain has become more sensitive.

Ronn Langford and I perform a dramatic demonstration of this fact in one of our Inner Speed Secrets seminars. As part of a demonstration of the importance of sensory input, and for a little lighthearted fun, we ask two participants to compete in a race. Not a car race, though. The competition is to see who can pull on a pair of women's knee-high nylons in the least amount of time, while blindfolded and wearing thick ski gloves. As you can imagine, with no visual input and very little kinesthetic input, this is a real challenge (and a few laughs for the rest of us).

Ronn and I had become quite accustomed to how long it takes a person to complete the competition. Then, in one particular seminar, a participant completed it in less than half the time it normally takes. It seemed as though he was pulling on the nylons without the gloves. It wasn't until the end of our little race that the participant reminded us that he was a dental surgeon, and worked all day long at very delicate maneuvers while wearing gloves. To him, even through the thick ski gloves, he had some sensitivity. That sensitivity had been developed through years of working while wearing gloves.

If you were to practice driving with very thick driving gloves, and then switched to ones that allowed more sensitivity when it came time to really perform (such as in qualifying or the race), your kinesthetic sensitivity would be enhanced. Therefore, your performance would improve.

The real point is, again, that your sensory input can be improved and developed, and that the more it is developed, the more sensitivity you will have to control your race car at the limit. The key is to practice being aware. Many people go through life without really being aware of what is going on around them—what they can really see, feel, hear, smell, and taste.

## Auditory Input

The same is true of your auditory sense. Try practicing while using heavy-duty ear plugs, which greatly restricting your auditory input. Then, go back to your regular ear plugs and notice how much more auditory input you receive.

Imagine driving your race car with overly effective ear plugs, ones that blocked out almost all the sound. You are driving the track, shifting up and down through the gears, the engine revving, the tires growling, the brakes grinding. But, you can barely hear all this auditory activity. You strain to hear the engine, having to rely more on the tachometer than you have in a long time to determine when to shift. There is auditory data going into your brain, just not as much as usual. You strain your hearing again to take in as much as possible.

By the end of the session you have your driving rhythm back, you've learned to adapt to the lack of auditory input. The fact is, your brain is extremely adaptable. In that short session, it has learned to perform nearly at the same level as before you restricted your auditory input. It has learned to be more sensitive.

Now, get back in the car for the next session, but this time with your regular ear plugs. These restrict the noise just enough to protect your hearing from damage, but still allow an abundance of auditory input. In fact, you may not have even realized how much sensory input you took in through your hearing before. But now you do. You are hearing the crispness of the engine's throttle response like never before. You had never noticed that sound from the tires before as you cross the concrete patch through the middle of the corner. What does that tell you about the tires's grip level? It changed, didn't it?

Wow! What a session! What a performance! You were magic in the car. It was as if things just happened, you didn't need to try to go fast. It was easy. That's what happens when you crank up the boost on just one of your sensory inputs.

Again, what you are doing is forcing your brain to work with restricted sensory input. Then, when it is used to constructing the information with little data input, give it back all the sensory input you can when it really counts.

A word of warning here, a serious one. Driving a race car, or just hanging around the track, without adequate hearing protection is a big mistake. In just a very short amount of time you can permanently damage your hearing. And you should now know just how much your driving performance will be negatively affected if your auditory input is reduced. So, don't get any ideas of heading out on to the track with little or no hearing protection!

## Speed Sensing

Speed sensing, particularly as it applies to the entry phase of a corner, covers a couple of areas. First, it is having the innate ability to accurately determine the ideal speed to slow the car to when entering a turn. Now, understand this does not mean knowing the car has to be traveling at 88.3 miles per hour when you reach the turn-in point. Obviously that wouldn't do you any good, as it is not possible to look at a speedometer when you are just about to enter a turn. That is why I say it has to be an innate sense.

The second area is the ability to consistently adjust the car's speed to the appropriate level for entering a turn. Just knowing deep down inside how fast you should be entering the corner doesn't help if you cannot tell the difference between 88.3 and 82.1 miles per hour. Great race drivers can sense the difference in speed within one mile per hour. The superstars are far more sensitive than that. And they can consistently dial the car into that speed.

Over the next few chapters, I will talk a bit more about the importance of speed sensing as it applies specifically to corner entry, mid-corner, and exit speed.

## Speed Sensing Exercise

Developing your speed sensing abilities is not an easy thing to do without miles and miles of track time. However, there are a couple of exercises I've come up with that will enhance and speed up the process of developing them.

The first is done in your street car on the street. All you are going to do is practice estimating speed, based simply on sensory input and not the speedometer. Cut out a piece of cardboard that you can easily slip in place to cover the speedometer, then go for a drive. As you are driving along at say, 55 miles per hour, slip the cardboard cover in place. Then change your speed a few times by speeding up and slowing down, and finally by trying to put the car back to 55 miles per hour again. Pull the cardboard cover off and check to see how accurate you are. Do it again and again.

An alternative method is to simply leave the cardboard cover in place and pick a speed you want to travel at. Then, accelerate to what you feel is that speed, and pull the cover off and check how well you did.

If you do these exercises over and over again, you will become very accurate, and most important, consistent at judging and establishing a specified speed. And no, it doesn't really matter that you are not at the same speed you will be at on the racetrack. The main objective to consistently set the speed of the car the same over and over again, within 1 mile per hour or so, simply using sensory input as your guide. That is accurate and consistent speed sensing.

Another technique to improve your speed sensing abilities requires a radar gun, someone to operate it, and you driving your race car. Choose the most important corner on the track, and have your assistant with the radar gun positioned so that he can check your speed just as you turn into the corner (using a pylon or pavement marker as a reference point). Take a couple of laps to warm up, and then drive ten laps with the main goal of entering the turn at exactly the same speed. Of course, it does no good to drive slowly during this exercise. You should be within a couple of tenths of your best lap times. Have your assistant radio to you the speed you were traveling as you turned into the corner.

The goal, of course, is to consistently be at the same speed as you turn in to the corner. If your corner entry speed varies more than 1 mile per hour, you really need to practice this more. Ultimately, you should be able to enter every corner on a racetrack at the same speed for at least ten laps in a row, within 1 mile per hour.

Your assistant should then ask you to increase your corner entry speed by 2 miles per hour. See if you know what that small increase feels like. Try 1 mile per hour less—how does that feel? The objective is to calibrate your speed sensing with reality. If you determine that increasing your Turn 3 corner-entry speed by 1 mile per hour is desirable, now you will have a better idea of what that feels like. You will have a better chance of going and doing that—not increasing your entry speed by 4 miles per hour, but by the 1 mile per hour you wanted.

Of course, this can also be done with a data acquisition system, although the feedback is delayed. The lack of instant feedback is certainly a drawback; with instant feedback, your mind learns quicker. The real-time feedback from an assistant is more effective.

## Traction Sensing

Traction sensing skill is one of the key differences between a truly great driver and all the rest.

To be able to drive at the limit and to use every bit, but not any more, of the tires' traction, you must be able to feel or sense how much traction the tires have. I know that sounds pretty obvious, but that is what traction sensing is: The ability to sense at any and all points around the racetrack exactly how much traction the car has. Or, put another way, it is the ability to sense if and when the car is at the traction limit.

The one question I'm asked more than just about any other by new and relatively new race drivers is, how can I tell exactly when I'm driving at the limit? It is perhaps the most difficult question

*Perhaps the single most important skill you must develop to be quick in a race car is traction sensing—the ability to sense exactly how much traction each tire has, and then use it all.*

to answer, for knowing precisely when you are driving at the limit is, besides being the key to driving at the limit, an innate feel that one develops. I don't believe it is something that a person is born with. Yes, some drivers seem to have a more natural feel or instinct for it, but with any driver, it can and must be developed.

Where does this ability to sense how much traction the tires have come from? Primarily from your senses, and specifically your senses of feel, vision, and hearing.

By simply being aware of the tires' traction all the time, including when you are driving on the street, your traction sensing skills will improve. In addition, there are a few specific exercises you can use to develop your traction sensing skills.

## Traction Sensing Exercises

Perhaps the best all-around exercise for developing your raw traction sensing skills is still a skid pad. For all the money that drivers and teams spend on practicing and testing, it seems ridiculous that little, if any, is spent on something as simple and effective as skid pad training.

As part of my development program for a Toyota Atlantic driver I worked with one year, we did a skid pad session. Although it was rather short, it was one of the most beneficial bits of training we did. The driver's understanding of how to control understeer and oversteer was really enhanced, as was his traction sensing sensitivity. You may be thinking that you fully understand how to control understeer and oversteer already, and that may be true. So did this driver. But it is not until you physically practice adjusting the throttle and steering input over and over that you truly understand it. Overall, I would estimate that his car control skills improved by at least 50 percent after that one skid pad session.

You do not need a full-blown skid pad to do this type of training. As we did with the Atlantic driver, all you require is a large, smooth, paved parking lot, some way of wetting it down (we hired a water tank truck to intermittently spray the area), and some cones. Set the cones up to form a circle at least 50 feet across. Then drive your race car around the circle faster and faster until either the front or rear tires begin to lose traction. On a skid pad like this, you should be able to hold the car in a steady-state understeer or oversteer slide for at least three or four laps of the circle. In other words, you should be able to keep the car in an oversteer drift, with

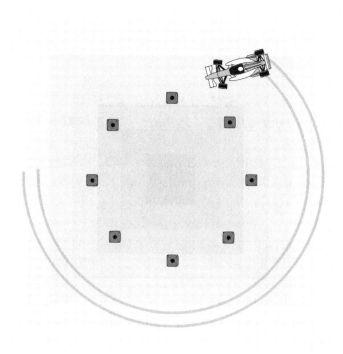

*You can set up a makeshift skid pad in a large paved parking lot to develop your traction sensing and car control skills. Use eight or more cones to describe a circle at least 50 feet in diameter, then add water, and go out and play . . . I mean practice.*

the tail hanging out and you controlling it with the throttle and steering lap after lap. The same is true with understeer.

To make this exercise most effective, it may be necessary to fiddle with the car a bit. I've gone as far as running rain tires on the front and slicks on the rear, and vice versa. Usually, though, just adjusting or disconnecting anti-roll bars is enough. Your objective is to be able to exaggerate the car's ability to understeer and oversteer.

As anyone who has read my previous two books knows, I am a big believer in using street driving to develop your race driving skills. And, you don't need to be driving at anywhere near racetrack speeds to do this. In fact, driving fast often defeats the purpose of what you are trying to accomplish. Unless you are driving at speed, at the limit, the correlation between street and track is not there. And only an idiot would drive that fast on the street. What you are trying to do is program specific skills and techniques in a relaxed, unhurried atmosphere. That way, when you are on the track, these skills and techniques come naturally, without any conscious thought whatsoever.

### SPEED SECRET #15:
### Use your street driving to make you a better track driver.

One of the first things you can do while driving on the street to enhance your traction sensing skills is simply to make note of the tires' traction. Do this by paying attention to the noise coming from them and by the feeling through the steering wheel. Notice how both these factors change when going from a straight line to cornering. Yes, on the street, the noise and feel will be minute, subtle things. But, if you can read the tire traction at this level, sensing it at racetrack speeds will be easy.

I'd like you to try an experiment for me. While driving on the street, try holding the steering wheel with a tight grip, with your whole hands wrapping around the wheel rim so that your palm is in contact with the wheel. Notice the vibrations back through the wheel. Next, hold the steering wheel with just your fingers, with a light, relaxed touch. Now notice the vibrations through the wheel. Which provides the most feedback? In which way do you feel the most vibrations? With the light touch of the fingers on the wheel, right?

Does this tell you something about how you should hold the steering wheel? I hope so. If you practice holding the steering wheel in your street car with your fingers, with a light touch, that will become a habit, a program. Yes, I know that some race cars require more of a grip of the wheel than what just your fingers can apply. But, if you make a light touch a habit, you will apply the lightest touch possible on your race car steering wheel. And that will lead to increased sensitivity and increased traction sensing abilities.

In all the coaching I've done, there is one exercise that has made the single biggest improvement with the drivers I work with: traction sensing sessions. All you do with this exercise is dedicate part or all of a practice or test session to simply focusing on sensing the tires' traction. While driving on the race track, make note of the vibrations and feedback through the steering wheel—does the steering get lighter or heavier as the tires slide more? Make note of the sound coming from the tires. Do they make more or less noise as they slide more? Overall, how does the car feel as the tires begin to slide more and more? How much warning do the tires give before they start to slide too much? Forgetting practically everything else, especially lap times, practice reading how much traction the tires have around every inch of the track.

You may even want to put a 1 to 10 rating scale on it, with 10 being the very limit of traction just before the tires start to let go, and 1 being the grip they have while going down a straightaway. Then, as you drive around the track, you can actually call out to yourself the amount of traction the tires have.

### *Speed Secret #16:*
### *Regularly use traction sensing sessions to improve your ability to drive at the limit.*

If you use these techniques on a regular basis, I guarantee your traction sensing abilities will improve and that will lead to your ability to drive more consistently at the limit.

# Chapter 5

# Driving at the Limit

B efore I go any further, I want to define exactly what I mean by "driving at the limit." When I say "at the limit," I mean having all four tires of the car at a point along the slip angle versus traction graph where they are producing their maximum amount of traction. It is when the car is being driven at a speed dead in the middle between two extremes:

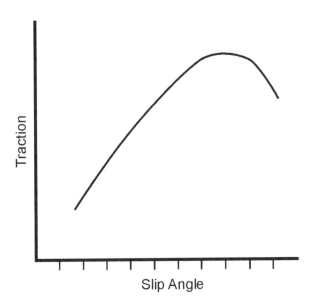

*This graph shows the relationship between your tires' slip angle and traction. As you can see, the greater the slip angle, the more traction the tires develop—up to a point, where the traction then begins to taper off.*

• At one extreme, the car is not being driven fast enough, and not all of the tires' traction is being used up. The car is being driven below the limit.

• At the other extreme, the car is being driven beyond the limit. The tires, and therefore the car, are sliding too much.

When I talk about "the limit," I'm not talking about some theoretical thing, mind you. No, I'm talking about the very real, physical limit or threshold of the tires gripping the track.

Although the limit is a very real, physical thing, it can change. That is, the way you drive the car will determine to some extent at what speed your tires and car reach the limit. That is why one driver can drive the car at the very limit, only to have another driver hop into the same car and go even faster. Was the first driver not driving the limit? He may very well have been. The point is, though, his driving technique may have produced a slightly lower limit than the second driver. How does that happen? Mostly by driving in such a way that the car is not as well balanced as it could be.

Of course, defining what driving at the limit is, and even doing it, is much easier than telling someone how to do it. Which is what I'm going to attempt to do in this book.

How do you really know when you are driving the car at a speed where all four tires are right at their limit of traction? Start by asking yourself some questions. Is the car sliding? If not, you can drive faster. Is the car sliding too much? If so, you are scrubbing off speed, and possibly overheating the tires. An excessive slide or drift may feel good, and look great, but it is usually not the quickest way around the track.

So, if no sliding is not enough, and too much is really too much, just how much is enough? And, how do you get there? Well . . . I could say that it just takes experience, seat time—honing in from too little to too much to just right. And, that's the start, but you didn't buy this book just to hear me say you need more seat time, so let me try to explain.

Most drivers, when they first begin racing, do not slide the car through the turns enough. It's like the car is on rails. Then, with experience, they begin to slide the car more and more, eventually learning to slide it too much—they are driving slightly beyond the limit. Finally, they learn to fine-tune the amount of sliding, homing in on the ideal slip angle.

As I said, the key is to keep the tires right at the peak of the slip angle versus tire traction curve. Without great traction sensing skills and awareness, you will never be able to tell when you are there and when you are

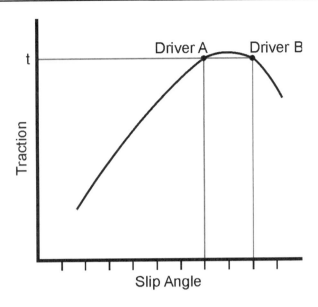

*Here are two drivers, Driver A and Driver B, on the same slip angle versus traction graph. Both drivers are generating the same level of traction (T), but Driver A is driving the car with seven degrees of slip angle, while Driver B is using nine degrees of slip angle. Both will turn the same lap time, as their cornering speeds will be the same, but Driver B has a bigger challenge: Driver B's point on the graph is less forgiving. If Driver A makes a small error, he will either be too slow or he will actually generate more traction. If Driver B makes a small error, he will either generate more traction or exceed the tires' traction limit and spin.*

on either side of the peak. And remember, we are not just talking about one part of a corner—for example, standing on the throttle exiting a turn with the car in an oversteer drift. No, we are talking about having all four tires at the ideal slip angle from the nanosecond that you turn into a corner to the exit point—every corner of every lap.

People talk about Michael Schumacher and how he just seems to be able to drive faster than everyone else. And yet, they don't talk about what he does to do that. Primarily, it is his ability to balance the car better than everyone else. Therefore, his limit is higher, as is his ability to sense the very peak of the tire traction curve and keep the car there.

When drivers ask me, "How do I know when I'm driving at the limit?," I immediately know one thing: They are trying to do too much at one time. The reason they don't know when they are at the limit is they are trying to drive the entire track or corner at the limit, all at once. A driver's mind is not capable of taking that much information in, and focusing on it, at one time. If the driver focused on driving at the limit in one phase, say, the exit only at first, then the entry, etc., he would be more successful at driving the limit.

Some people's response to the above question is, if you have to ask, you'll never be a real race driver. That's silly. These people either have never driven near the limit themselves or were one of the lucky ones who stumbled onto the strategy I suggest, without knowing that is what they are doing.

Of course, the other response is that you have to drive over the limit, to the point of spinning or crashing, and then dial it back a bit from there. In my way of thinking, that is the not the ideal way of reaching your goal. It is dangerous, expensive, and not the quickest way of learning since you will spend so much time getting your car back on track or repairing it.

The key is to have a strategy and specific objectives. Break the task down into manageable bites, and then focus on only two or three of them at a time.

## Bites at the Limit

Having spent most of my life studying the driving styles and techniques of thousands of drivers I have raced against, coached, or intently watched, I have come to the following conclusion. The art of driving a race car really fast—driving at the very limit—does not come from just one thing (which, I'm sure, surprises no one). No, when you break the craft of driving a race car down to the very basics, there are four separate, but related things that a driver must do to drive as fast as possible:

• Identify the ideal path or line around the racetrack and then drive the race car along it—the line

• drive the race car at the limit at the exit of every corner—through the exit phase

• drive the race car at the limit when entering every corner—through the entry phase

• drive the race car at the limit in the middle of every corner—through the mid-corner phase.

Simple and obvious enough! And by the way, these four stages are exactly what each and every driver, from novice to World Champion, naturally works on when trying to drive at the limit, in the order most drivers naturally approach it.

When someone first begins to drive race cars, the first thing they learn is how to determine and then drive the ideal line. As the driver gains a little more experience, he begins to work on the exit phase of the corner—getting on the throttle earlier and earlier to maximize the ensuing straightaway speed. In most cases, at the club and minor professional levels, the driver who drives the best line and gets on the throttle at the exit of the corner first wins most often.

Drivers at the upper levels of professional racing have all but perfected the line and the exit stages of driving, and now the difference between the winners and losers is all in the entry phase. Watch closely and observe the speed that the winner in a CART Champ Car race carries into the turns. He is definitely quicker than the drivers who do not win. For example, Juan Montoya was visibly quicker at the entry of every corner than the drivers finishing further back in the field. Yes, I know that some of it has to do with the car and its setup, but the driver is the final determining factor—and it's all in the corner entry speed.

*What it's all about: using up every fraction of an inch of track, driving the car at the limit at each and every piece of track.*

Finally, what separates the truly great drivers like Michael Schumacher from everyone else is the speed carried through the middle of the turns.

The ultimate objective of the first step, perfecting the ideal line, is obvious: Just drive the line around the track that minimizes the amount of time spent lapping the track. However, there are practically an infinite number of possible lines a driver could drive through a particular corner.

Combine that with the number of lines used to connect each and every turn on the track, and you begin to see the enormity and challenge of just this part of driving a race car.

If the only goal of selecting the ideal line was to maximize your speed through each individual corner, the job would only be difficult. But, each turn on the track cannot be considered in isolation. They are connected and often are affected by each other. And the line chosen will determine, to some extent, your success with the other three priorities: the exit, entry, and mid-corner speed.

Learning the line is the first step every race driver goes through, and it is often the difference between winning and losing in the early stages of a racing career. Let's just say it is highly doubtful that a driver is ever going to win if he hasn't figured out how to identify and drive the ideal line on a racetrack. Of course, this is the first area where a good driver coach can help you.

In terms of the exit phase of the corners, the ultimate goal is to begin your acceleration as early and as hard as the car can possibly take. This must still be done absolutely as smoothly as possible, otherwise it will delay the acceleration. And again, the line you have chosen will play a big factor in your exit phase.

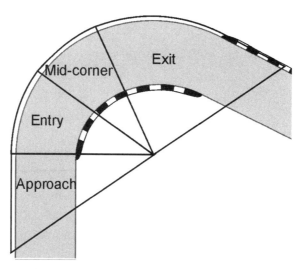

*By breaking your job of driving at the limit into manageable bites, the odds of consistently doing it are better. You should start by breaking each corner into phases: the approach, entry, mid-corner, and exit.*

Practically every race driver who wins races at the amateur or professional level has pretty much perfected the line and exit phases of race driving.

The one place where it is obvious that the real stars and champions outshine the rest is in the entry phase of the corners. They are able to carry more speed into the turns without negatively affecting the line or exit phase. Of course, any driver can carry lots of speed into a corner. The key is to be able to do it without it hurting your corner exit speed.

The key to the entry phase is carrying enough speed, but not too much. That is why this phase often separates the winners from the also-rans.

The last step in becoming a real superstar is the mid-corner phase. This is what separates Michael Schumacher, for example, from all the rest. Yes, I'm sure the entire F1 grid can drive as good a line as he does and can probably accelerate out of the turns as well as he does. And yes, a few others can carry as much speed into the turns as Schumacher. But that is where the similarities start to diminish. I wish it was easier to compare, but if you watch very carefully, you can see for yourself that he is able to consistently carry more speed through the middle of the corners than anyone else.

So, the driver who is going to be the quickest is the one who drives the ideal line, gets on the throttle the earliest and hardest exiting the turns, carries the most speed into these turns, and manages to maintain the momentum or speed through the middle of the corners. Simple enough (I wish!).

As I said, each and every one of these stages is related and interrelated. You can never think that once you have mastered one stage that you will never have to go back and work on it again. It is a constant game of getting one just right, only to have to modify it once you get another stage right, and then another, and so on.

No matter who the driver is, it is not just a matter of learning each step and then never having to go back to re-learn or improve one of the steps. In fact, it is a continual cycle. The driver learns the ideal line, then works on getting on the power earlier and earlier until the exit phase is under control. Then the driver works on maximizing his corner entry speed; and finally, on perfecting the mid-corner speed. At that point, the driver usually has to go back and alter the line slightly, which results in having to work on the exit phase again, then the entry and mid-corner again. Then the cycle starts all over.

In reality, it is not something that you will go through once, perfecting each stage at one shot and then moving on to the next. No, it is almost a continuous loop, sometimes not even going back to the beginning, but hopping around from one stage to another. In the beginning you will work on getting the line down just right, then accelerating early out of the corners, carrying more speed into the turns, and getting the mid-corner right. Then, it is possibly back to the line again, as all this focus on gaining speed in the other phases means altering the line slightly. Or, you may get the corner entry phase just right and then have to go back and work on getting back on the throttle early in the exit phase. Or, once the mid-corner speed is up, the entry phase needs work. In fact, it is an endless pursuit: the pursuit of the perfect corner, then the perfect lap, and ultimately the perfect race. Can it be done? Perhaps not. But the pursuit of it is the real challenge—and thrill.

The truly great drivers are doing this all the time—each and every lap they are on the track—whether they are consciously aware of doing it or

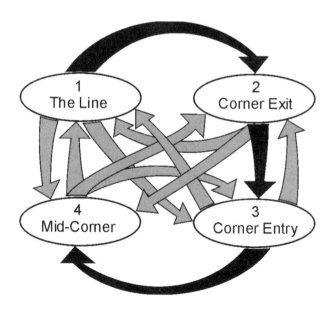

*There are four stages every driver goes through in learning to drive consistently at the very limit. But, as the illustration shows, once you've gone through each stage once, you should continually go back and fine-tune each one again and again. The learning never ends.*

not. For the greats, this whole process occurs at a subconscious level; a level where they are not having to actually think through what they are doing, they are just doing it.

How do you do that? How do you perfect each step, each piece of the puzzle? I hope to answer those questions over the next four chapters, as I attempt to explain what it takes to maximize your performance—and drive the car at the limit—in each of these four stages. Of course, I will only do that at a conscious level. I will help you become aware of what is required to drive at the limit. It will then be up to you to take that knowledge, that understanding of the process, and turn that into an ability to do it on the racetrack, at speed, at a subconscious level.

There may be times where you are looking for the last few tenths of a second in lap time, but you're not sure where it is going to come from. At this point, someone may suggest that it is not going to come from one place, but rather a tiny little bit from a few places; perhaps from each corner on the track. And they are right.

The key to finding the last few tenths most often comes from ensuring the car is being driven to the very limit—the ragged edge—in every segment of every turn on the track. Many drivers drive the car at the limit through one or two segments of a turn, for most of the corners. But they are not driving all three segments of every corner at the limit.

### SPEED SECRET #17:
### Drive the car at the very limit for every segment, for every turn, for every lap.

Before we go any further, I think it is important that you understand what exactly I mean by some very common terms.

### Turn-in

The term turn-in is used to describe what the car is doing during that fraction of a second that you initially turn the steering wheel at the beginning of a corner. Ultimately, you want the car's turn-in to be "crisp," meaning the car changes direction immediately when you turn the steering wheel. At the same time, the turn-in can be too crisp. The opposite of a crisp turn-in is a lazy turn-in. A lazy turn-in means there is some amount of delay from the time you turn the steering wheel until the time the car changes direction.

Of course, how *you* turn in is going to vary, as well, depending on the type of corner you're faced with. More about this in Chapter 8.

## Corner Entry

The entry of a corner is from just after the initial turn-in to the mid-corner section. Think of it as the section of the corner between the turn-in and the point in the corner where the car is in a steady state. In the corner entry phase, you are continuing the motion of winding in more steering input.

The entry phase can also be thought of as beginning just after turn-in and continuing until your right foot begins to apply some throttle.

## Mid-Corner

The mid-corner is usually when you have wound in all of the steering input required to get the car aimed toward the apex, and you are not yet unwinding the steering. The car is on a consistent radius: not decreasing, nor increasing. Some corners do not have a mid-corner phase, as the second you have dialed in enough steering to aim the car toward the apex, you immediately begin to unwind it toward the exit.

You can also use the throttle application to define the mid-corner: from the second your foot touches the throttle, to the point it begins to really "hammer down" (smoothly) on it. Therefore, the mid-corner may be non-existent if the second you touch the throttle you squeeze it all the way down. It may be very short if you have a brief period of time where you are using a maintenance throttle—not increasing or decreasing the throttle. Or, it could be relatively lengthy in a long, fast sweeper.

## Corner Exit

The exit of the corner is the section where you are unwinding the steering, increasing the radius of the line the car is following. Typically, it is from the apex to the exit or track-out point of the corner. Again, the exit phase is also defined as beginning when you begin squeezing the throttle down to wide open.

## Trail Braking

Braking can actually be broken down into approach braking and trail braking. Approach braking is just as it sounds, the braking you do on the approach to the corner. The second you begin to turn the steering wheel into the corner, approach braking ends. Trail braking begins as soon as approach braking ends, at the turn-in point. It is the physical act of easing, or trailing your foot off the brake pedal. Where you finish trail braking, and how much you trail brake, is entirely dependent on the specific corner, the type of car you are driving, and your driving style.

I know there are some people who say they never trail brake. Some racing schools actually teach this and say a driver should never trail brake. They are dead wrong. Every successful driver trail brakes to some extent in some corners. I'll deal with this in more detail in Chapter 7.

### Off-Throttle

In theory, you should never be coasting in a race car—you should either be braking or applying the throttle. In reality, coasting is sometimes (although rarely) necessary. Any moment where you are neither braking or applying the throttle, you are coasting or off-throttle.

### Maintenance Throttle

This is where you are not accelerating, nor decelerating, you are simply maintaining your speed. Think of it in terms of driving down a highway at a constant 55 miles per hour. Not all corners and cars require maintenance throttle—you may directly and immediately go from off the throttle while braking to squeezing down the throttle, accelerating out of the corner. Some cars and corners require a very short period of maintenance throttle.

### Acceleration

Accelerating is when you are progressively increasing the speed of the car by either squeezing down on the throttle or holding it to the floor.

# Chapter 6

# *The Line*

I want to start the discussion on how to master the line with a reasonably obvious piece of physics—perhaps, something that you are at least subconsciously aware of: corner speed is proportional to corner radius.

What does this really mean? Simply that the more speed you carry through a corner, the larger the radius of the turn must be. Alternatively, the tighter the radius of the corner, the slower you must drive. Simple enough, right? And, like I said, even if this is something you had not consciously thought of before, I'm sure you knew this at the intuitive or subconscious level.

Of course, I'm talking here about driving at the limit the entire way through the turn with the tires at their very limit before breaking loose and beginning to slide.

Now, let's take this physics discussion a step further. As you also know at the intuitive level, the tighter the radius or the faster you drive through a corner, the more you feel the g-forces—the more g-forces the

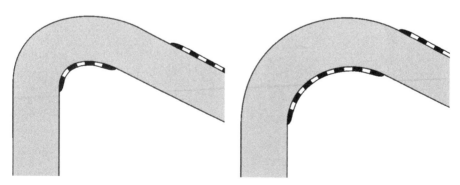

*Which corner do you think you can drive through the fastest? Right, the one with the largest radius. The same theory applies to the line you drive: the larger the radius or arc you follow, the faster you can drive.*

car is generating. Again, I know you know what a g-force is from an intuitive point of view, but what does it really mean?

G-force is the lateral force acting on the car and you while going around a corner, with 1.0 g being equal to the force of gravity pushing laterally (sideways) on the car.

Speed is proportional to corner radius, and the faster you drive or the tighter the radius of the turn, the higher the g-forces. Now, let's put these two facts together into one mathematical statement: $S = g/R$ (where S represents speed in miles per hour, g is lateral g-force, and R is the radius of the corner in feet). In other words, the speed you can drive through a corner is proportional to the amount of g-force generated, divided by the corner radius.

What does this really mean, and why do you need to know this? Actually, you probably don't need to know the actual physics and math that goes along with this. What you do need to know, and what this really means, is that the speed you drive through any particular turn is determined by the g-force your car is capable of generating—which is determined by the mechanical and aerodynamic grip the car has, along with your ability to balance the car to maximize the tires' grip and the radius of the corner.

In terms of your driving then, there are two areas you can work on to maximize your speed: balancing the car (to maximize tire traction) and increasing the radius of the corner. I'll discuss balancing the car in the sections on corner exit, entry and mid-corner. For now, let's look at the corner radius.

Driving through a turn using the largest possible radius means following what we call the "geometric line." This is the line that you would draw with a compass, using up every inch of the track surface, from outside edge to inside edge and back out to the outside again, on a constant radius. See the illustration at left.

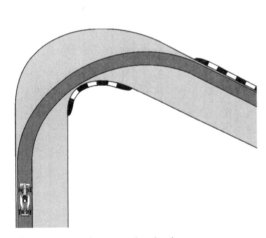

*The geometric line may be the fastest way to drive through one corner in isolation, but it isn't necessarily the fastest way around the track.*

Before going any further, I need to review something I talked about in *Speed*

*Secrets.* If you decrease the radius of a turn by not using all the track, your maximum speed will be significantly reduced. For example, by entering a corner even one foot away from the edge of track, the radius of the turn may be reduced by as much as 1 percent. What's 1 percent worth? As much as half a second on some road racing circuits. What's half a second worth to you? From this I'm sure you see how critical using every inch of track surface really is.

Back to our geometric line. Although the geometric line is the fastest way to drive through each particular turn, it is not the fastest way of getting around the entire track. The reason for this has to do with the fact that there is usually something following the turns that is more important: the straightaways. If you have driven at least one race in your life, I'm sure you already know that it is far easier to pass a competitor on the straights than it is in the turns. What may not be so obvious at times is that there is more time to be gained, resulting in lower lap times, by being fast on the straightaways. In other words, it is far more important to be fast on the straights than it is to be fast in the corners.

Obviously, that doesn't mean putt-putting around the turns at a crawl. What it does mean is driving the turns in such a way as to maximize your straightaway speed. And that means altering the line you drive from the geometric line to one that allows for earlier acceleration, one we call the "ideal line." In most cases, that means driving a line with a later turn-in, apex, and exit. See the illustration below for an example.

*Driving the ideal line (the white striped line) does mean you will have to enter the corner a little slower—due to the tighter initial radius—but it allows you to begin accelerating earlier, which will result in faster speeds on the following straight. Also, you spend less overall time cornering and more time braking and accelerating.*

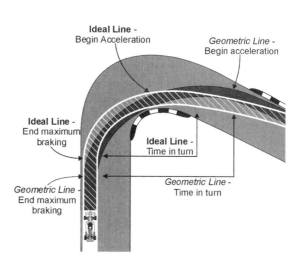

The benefits of a line with a later turn-in, apex and exit are:

1. You spend less overall time in the corner. When do you have the most control over your car—when you are on the straight or in the corner? And, didn't we already decide that the larger the radius the faster we could drive? Less time in the corner equals more time on the straight—or at least near straight—which is about as large a radius as you can find.

2. You are able to begin accelerating earlier. The sooner you get back on the throttle and begin accelerating out of a corner, the faster you will be down the ensuing straightaway.

3. You can maintain your speed on the approaching straightaway longer by braking slightly later. Because you are turning into the corner later, the straightaway approaching the turn has effectively become longer, and therefore, you can maintain your speed longer.

4. By turning into the corner a little later, it allows you to see around the turn better. On most road racing circuits, this is not a big benefit—your vision is not blocked anyway—but on street circuits in particular, with the cement walls on the inside of the turn, it can make a big difference.

However, along with those benefits comes a negative. In this case, due to the later turn-in, your line through the early part of the turn is a tighter radius. You know what that means—lower speed. But, this trade-off is an easy decision. Yes, you have to go a little slower early in the corner, but you more than make up for it down the following straight by beginning to accelerate earlier.

Now that I've convinced you of the benefits of using a late apex in each and every corner, think about something. Does this analysis of turns, and the resulting late apex line, work for every corner? Not necessarily. Let me give you a general rule, a very general rule:

### SPEED SECRET #18:
### *The faster the corner, the closer to the geometric line you should drive; the slower the corner, the more you need to alter your line with a later apex.*

Let's take a good look at why this is the case.

**Change of Speed.** Remember that phrase. The greater the potential for change of speed from corner entry to corner exit, the straighter you want your car pointed to allow for acceleration. In other words, the slower the corner, the later the apex you should use. A corner taken in first or second gear is certainly going to allow a greater change of speed than one taken in fourth or fifth gear, so you would use a later apex in the former than you would in the latter.

Based on what you now know about corner radius versus speed, you could also interpret my general rule as: The tighter the radius, the later the apex; the larger the radius, the earlier the apex, or the closer to a geometric line. In simple terms, a slow hairpin will require a later apex than a fast, sweeping turn.

Once again, the reason has to do with your change of speed. In a hairpin turn you will be accelerating hard out of the corner and your change in speed will be relatively high. Your change of speed through a high-speed turn will not be so high, due to your car's reduced ability to accelerate the faster you are traveling. If that does not make sense, ask yourself this question: Can my car accelerate from 100 to 110 miles per hour as quickly as it can from 50 to 60 miles per hour? The obvious answer is "no." Any car, no matter how much engine torque it has, can accelerate quicker in the lower gears than in the higher gears.

So, a general theme or objective in slower corners is to turn-in and apex late, which allows the car to be driven on an increasing radius (a straighter line) when heavy acceleration is required. In faster corners,

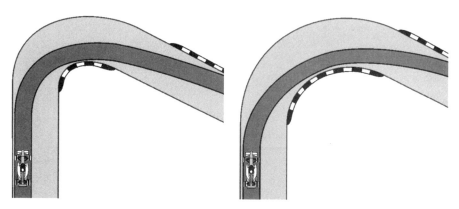

*Compare the apex point in these corners. The one on the left, with the smaller, or tighter, radius, uses a later apex than the larger radius turn. As a general rule, the larger the radius of the corner, the earlier the apex. Why? Because you don't have to rely so much on accelerating hard out of the turn, since the larger radius allows you to maintain more speed through the corner.*

where acceleration is limited anyway, you want to use an earlier turn-in and apex, allowing you to maintain or carry more speed into the turn.

The other factor to consider here is how sharply you have to make the initial turn-in. Obviously, to turn-in and apex later in the corner, you have to drive a sharper radius early in the turn. And you know what that means. Slower speed. In faster corners, the initial turn-in will be less sharp, allowing you to carry more speed.

Using a later turn-in and apex requires a significantly different speed of turning the steering wheel and a different amount and timing of trail braking than a fast corner's turn-in technique. I will revisit this concept in Chapter 8 when I discuss corner entry.

## G-force Junkies

Most people who race or are involved in any type of performance driving—myself included—are what I call "g-force junkies." We are addicted to g-forces, that feeling of being pushed sideways or backwards in the seat, or forced up against the seatbelts. The more g-force, the better. For those who are competing on a race track, at least, that is usually a good thing, because as we saw earlier, the more g-force, the faster we are moving. However, that is not always the case. In fact, there are really two ways to feel more g-force:

• Increase your speed, which is one of the objectives of race driving the last time I checked!

• Reduce the radius of the corner: The tighter the line around a corner, the more g-force you will feel. But what's wrong with that? Every time you decrease the radius of the corner, you have to reduce your speed, which certainly isn't the objective.

So to satisfy your g-force addiction, you may, without even being consciously aware of it, begin to tighten up the radius of a corner. Or, at least, not drive in such a way as to lessen the g-forces. Where this often shows up is at the exit of a corner, in not unwinding the steering wheel and releasing the car out of the turn. I will talk more about this in the corner exit chapter.

The ultimate goal is to only increase g-forces by increasing your speed. In fact, one of the goals of driving the ideal line is to minimize g-forces so that you can then increase them by increasing your speed.

Again, we come back to this compromise: increase the radius of the turn and we can drive faster through the corner. But, the more we alter the line toward a late turn-in/apex (a tighter radius early in the corner), the sooner we can begin accelerating and the faster we will be down the straightaway. Finding the ultimate compromise, the ideal line, for each and every turn on every track you race on is the challenge and is one of the biggest challenges of race driving.

## Prioritizing Corners

There are three important reasons for prioritizing the various corners on a racetrack:

1. When you are learning a track, it is very difficult (if not impossible) to try to learn every corner all at once. It is much easier to work on one or two corners at a time, moving on to the next when you feel you are doing a good job with the previous. When you know which corners are most critical to your overall lap times, you can concentrate on getting them right first.

2. There are times when you must compromise the car's setup to suit one corner more than another. In this case, it is best to set the car up for the most important corners.

3.) Even when you know a racetrack very well, you should constantly be trying to find some new or different approach to your driving technique that results in more speed. When doing that, sometimes you may have to compromise one turn's speed for another. If you know which corners are most important, you know which ones can be compromised and which ones can't.

There are two ways of looking at which corners on the track are the most important. The first is which corner is most beneficial to producing the quickest lap time; the second is which is the most challenging.

The old rule was the corner leading onto the longest straight was the most important in terms of your lap time. Then, in *Speed Secrets,* I updated that by saying the most important corner on the track is the fastest one leading onto a long straight. After all, some tracks have straightaways of almost equal length—which then is the most important corner? And, even though a 40 mile per hour hairpin may lead onto a straight that is a little longer than another corner that can be taken at 80 miles per hour, improvement in the faster corner will result in the greatest gain in speed. So, it is not as simple as just determining which corner is followed by the longest straight.

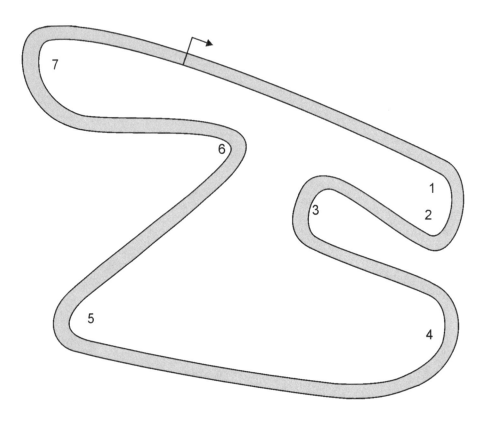

*Looking at this track map, which turn is the most important corner? Is it Turn 7, the one leading onto the longest straightaway? Or is it Turn 4, the fastest corner leading onto a long straightaway? Right, Turn 4. Which is the least important corner on the track? Probably Turn 2 or 3.*

### SPEED SECRET #19:
### *Focus on the most important corner first; and lastly the least important.*

The corner that is the most challenging or difficult can also be the most important turn. Usually, the most difficult corner will give you your greatest improvement in lap time. Why? Simply because that is the corner that you are most likely to be farthest away from having "perfected." And, of course, if it is challenging to you, it probably is to your competitors as well. That means that if you can perfect it, you will have gained the most on the drivers you are racing against.

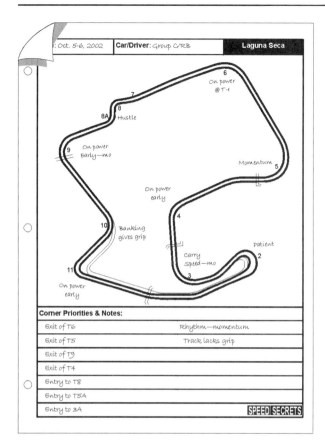

| Oct. 5-6, 2002 | **Car/Driver:** Group C/RB | Laguna Seca |

On power @ T-1

Hustle

On power Early—mo

Momentum

On power early

Banking gives grip

Carry Speed—mo

Patient

On power early

**Corner Priorities & Notes:**

| Exit of T6 | Rhythm—momentum |
| Exit of T5 | Track lacks grip |
| Exit of T9 | |
| Exit of T4 | |
| Entry to T8 | |
| Entry to T5A | |
| Entry to 3A | SPEED SECRETS |

*Prior to going to a track, sit down and write out what the track's corner priorities are, along with any other notes, thoughts, or ideas you may have about driving the track.*

## The Line You Drive

Late turn-in and apex, early turn-in and apex, mid-turn-in and apex. Which one do you use? Of course, there is no one answer to that question. Ultimately, it is up to you to figure it out.

If you've been driving on racetracks for some time now, you drive the line you do either because someone told you to, or because it just feels right.

Obviously, if you are driving a line through a corner because of the first reason, let's hope the person who told you knew what he was talking about. If not, you're in trouble and you had better find someone else for advice. This is why I suggest you also use the second reason to determine your line. Sure, having someone you trust give you an idea of where you need to be is okay for starters, but you had better move on to what feels right very soon.

Does that mean that you cannot go wrong with the "it feels right" method; that it will always result in the perfect line? Absolutely not! In fact, very often, a not-so-perfect line will feel good, at least if you rely on only one of your senses for that "feel." For example, many drivers turn in early for corners because it visually "feels right." They look to the apex at the inside of the corner and naturally turn the steering wheel to go there. So visually it looks right, but about the moment the outside tires are dropping off the edge of the track at the exit, kinesthetically it does not feel so good (sometimes referred to as the "pucker factor")!

It is when you use all three sensory inputs to "feel" what's right that the car will tell you what line to drive. And, it will do that in a very obvious way. It won't be subtle. It will be very direct. But only if you pay attention. And by paying attention, I mean being very sensitive to what you see, what you feel, and what you hear. If you don't understand exactly what I'm talking about, go back and re-read Chapter 4.

# Chapter 7

# The Exit Phase

This is one of the shorter chapters in this book. Why? Mostly because I assume that anyone reading this book has already gotten themselves to the point with their driving technique, their skills, and abilities, where the corner exit phase is relatively fine-tuned. It's an area that is as close to being perfectable as one ever gets in driving a race car. If not, you are going to have to go back to the basics.

The goal for the exit phase of any corner can be summed up best by the following statement: The driver who begins accelerating first will arrive at the other end of the straightaway—and most times the finish line—first. That is what the exit phase of corners is all about—maximizing your acceleration down the following straightaway. But, there are limits.

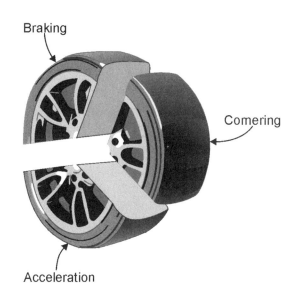

Braking

Comering

Acceleration

*A tire can be used to do three things: brake, corner, and/or accelerate. You can use all of the tire's traction for one of these, or combine two of the forces at one time, within limits.*

## The 100 Percent Tire Rule

As I'm sure you already know, a tire's traction can be used for braking, cornering, accelerating, or some combination of these three. In fact, you can use 100 percent of the tires' traction for braking. You can use 100 percent for cornering. Or, you can use 100 percent for accelerating. But you cannot use 100 percent for cornering and 100 percent for accelerating at the same time. You can't even use 1 percent for accelerating if you are using 100 percent for cornering. You can only get 100 percent out of the tires, not any more than that.

I spent a fair bit of time discussing this topic in *Speed Secrets*, particularly in relation to the traction circle. The key point I want to make or reiterate is that overlapping your braking, cornering, and accelerating, without asking for more than 100 percent from the tires, is critical to going fast. It is your ultimate goal.

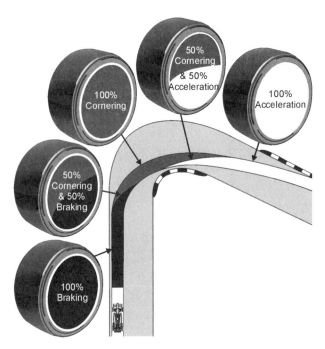

*You can only get 100 percent out of a tire, whether you are braking, cornering, accelerating, or doing some combination of the three. The driver that consistently uses all 100 percent and no more will most often be the quickest. Some drivers try to get more than 100 percent from their tires and crash a lot; others never ask enough of their tires—90 to 95 percent—and are slow.*

To drive at the limit, you must use all of the tires' traction throughout the track. As you begin braking for a corner, use 100 percent of the traction for braking. When you reach the turn-in point and begin to turn the steering wheel, you must ease off the brakes, trading some of the braking traction for cornering traction and going from a combination of 100 percent braking/0 percent cornering, through 50 percent braking/50 percent cornering, to 0 percent braking/100 percent cornering. For some amount of time—ranging from a very small fraction of a second to a few seconds—all you are doing is cornering at 100 percent. Then, as you unwind the steering, you trade off cornering traction for acceleration traction.

### Speed Secret #20:
### You can only use 100 percent of the tires' traction, and make sure you do.

This is the key to the exit phase of a corner—unwinding the steering, or releasing the car out of the turn, and allowing you to use the tires' traction for accelerating. Because, as I said, the sooner you begin accelerating, the faster you will be down the straight.

Remember what I said about being a g-force junkie in the previous chapter? Often, to fill your need to feel g-forces, you will subconsciously hold the arc of a turn just a little longer than necessary. In other words, you don't unwind the steering and allow the car to follow an increasing radius. The longer you hold the car on a tight radius, the more g-forces you will feel, but the slower you will be able to drive. So, unwind the steering wheel and let the car run free!

If you constantly think about this concept and keep in mind the 100 percent tire rule, you will be more likely to consistently drive at the limit.

A quick but important point for driving on an oval track, or any road course corner with a concrete wall lining the track: the more you try to keep the car away from the wall at the exit, the more likely it is you will end up hitting it. Unwind the steering and let the car track-out as close to the wall as possible.

When and how you begin accelerating in a corner also plays a critical role in the exit phase. Again, the general rule is the sooner you begin accelerating, the better. However, with some cars you need to be a little patient getting back to power. If you begin to accelerate too soon, all you

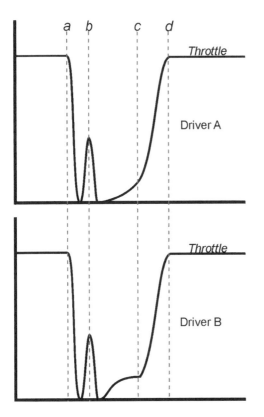

*Here's the throttle trace graph of two different drivers in the same corner. Both drivers come off the gas at the same point at the end of the straightaway (a); and they both blip the throttle for a downshift at the same spot (b). But notice the difference in how they get back on the throttle. Driver A in the top graph does a nice job of squeezing back on the throttle; Driver B does something a little different: He picks up the throttle a little earlier, then squeezes fully on. In most cases (but not all), Driver B's throttle application will result in a quicker lap time. Many times, this early touch of the throttle also helps balance the car and improves mid-corner speed.*

do is unload the front tires, causing the car to understeer, and then you have to ease back off the throttle to control it.

With other cars, almost from the instant you turn in to the corner you need to begin squeezing back on the throttle, and quickly. You need to experiment with your car to find out what works in each and every corner.

One more thing to keep in mind. For every inch of track surface you leave by not letting the car run out to the edge, you are giving speed away. If your outside tires are not at least nibbling at the curbing, riding on top of the curbing, or hanging the outside half an inch of them over the edge of the track, you will not be as fast as you could be. Do you get my hint?

### SPEED SECRET #21:
### *Every inch of track you are not using is costing you speed. You paid for it, so use it all.*

# Chapter 8

# *The Entry Phase*

Compared to the exit phase of a corner, the entry phase is usually much more challenging. Paul van Valkenburgh once said the skill required to squeeze down on the throttle, keeping the tires at the very limit of adhesion while accelerating out of a corner, is like walking a tightrope, while the skill required to determine and set the car's speed when entering a turn is like jumping onto a tightrope blindfolded.

While technically the entry phase begins only at the turn-in point, I will also discuss the corner approach—braking and downshifting—in this chapter.

One of the first pieces of advice that new race drivers are given is that going into the corners slowly and coming out fast is better than the opposite. Although this advice is entirely true, some drivers take this too far. This advice may cause some drivers to be slow. Why? Because many drivers do not carry enough speed into the corners.

Ultimately, you want to carry more and more speed into the corner until it begins to negatively affect when you can begin to accelerate. If your corner entry speed is so high that you have to delay the point where you begin to accelerate, then you need to slow down on the entry.

Let's look at a couple of examples to see what happens when your corner entry speed is not ideal. First, imagine entering a turn 1 or 2 miles per hour too fast. Although that is not much too fast, it will definitely delay the time when you can get back to throttle and begin accelerating. As I said, if your corner entry speed negatively affects when you can begin to accelerate, you need to enter slightly slower. Corner exit speed is usually more important than entry speed.

Having said that, imagine entering a corner 1 or 2 miles per hour *slower* than ideal. What happens then? One of two things. First, and probably the lesser of the two evils, is you have lost momentum, and momentum is always important. Whether you are driving a 60 horsepower Formula Vee or a 900 horsepower Champ car, every time you slow the car down it takes some amount of time to accelerate back up to speed again. If you slow the car more than necessary, it will take time to get that speed back, while in the meantime your competitors are probably pulling away from you.

The second and more damaging—and more difficult to recognize— effect of over-slowing your car for a corner is what I call the change of speed problem (there's that phrase again). I will discuss this in detail a bit later in this chapter, but the basic idea is that if you over-slow the car on the entry, you will naturally want to accelerate hard to get back up to speed. This acceleration will often result in a form of power oversteer in rear-wheel-drive cars, and power-understeer in front-wheel drive cars.

*Your corner entry is absolutely critical. If you over-slow the car by even 1 mile per hour, you may never be able to make up for that error, no matter how much horsepower your car has.*

You can see from these examples just how critical getting the exact right speed is when entering a corner. To do this, you need accurate and sensitive traction sensing skills. It also requires very finely tuned speed sensing skills. I talked about how to enhance and improve both your speed and traction sensing skills in Chapter 4. In addition to these skills, there are a few techniques that may improve your corner entry speed.

## Left-foot Braking

Over the past few years, it has become obvious that if you want to win in any form of racing that uses purpose-built race cars (F1, Champ car, Indy Lights, Formula Atlantic, Prototype Sports cars, Formula Ford), you must left-foot brake. Why is that, and what has changed to make that statement so true?

At one time, some of these race cars had gearboxes that rewarded the use of the clutch. That is not the case anymore. Most now feature a sequential-shift operation. The point is you do not need to use the clutch to shift. Not only do you not need it, it will actually slow your shifts if you do.

Of course, the main reason for this change in technique being used by today's winning drivers has to do with their backgrounds. Most of the top drivers today have spent many years racing karts. And what do you do with your feet in a kart? It's right foot on the gas, and left foot on the brake pedal. It's the years and years of training the left foot to be sensitive that results in great left-foot braking in race cars later in the career.

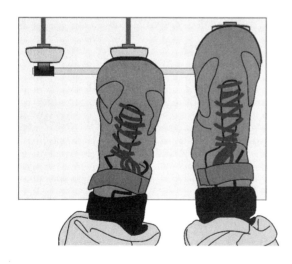

*Left-foot braking is one technique that you will need to develop if you want to make it in Formula One, Indy car, or NASCAR.*

If a driver has not spent many years using his left foot for braking in a kart, the driver may never acquire the accuracy and sensitivity to left-foot brake at the level required. And, that practicing may have to take place at an early age to become a well-programmed, subconscious technique. Why? In his book, *Why Michael Couldn't Hit,* neurologist Dr. Harold L.

Klawans sheds some light on why Michael Jordan could not hit a baseball well enough to make it in the major leagues during his hiatus from basketball. The bottom line, according to Klawans, is that if a physical technique has not had some programming by the early to mid-teen years, the brain and body will never be able to produce the psychomotor skill necessary to perform at the highest levels. In other words, Michael didn't hit enough baseballs as a kid.

The following article written by Matt Bishop in the June 8, 2000 issue of *Autosport* magazine puts the left-foot braking issue into a F1 perspective:

If there is one hour in the whole F1 season that sorts the men from the boys, it's qualifying at Monte Carlo. Last Saturday, the front-row stars of this white-knuckle hour were Michael Schumacher and Jarno Trulli. Michael, we know about. But what can we learn from Jarno's dazzling performance? Good question. And we'll come back to it.

Three laps into last year's race, Damon Hill exited the tunnel, braked for the chicane, got it wrong, and lightly punted his Jordan into the barrier. I was standing at the swimming pool complex at the time, and 10 minutes later a stern-faced Damon strode into view. He walked 20 yards past me, then stopped. There he stayed, silent, for 10 minutes more, watching the cars speed past.

At the next race, I asked him what he had seen. "I stood at Tabac," he told me, "but I couldn't really tell anything because the barriers were too high. So I went to the entrance of the swimming pool, the fast left-right, and you could start to see something. Michael (Schumacher) and Mika (Hakkinen)—but particularly Michael—were going through way quicker.

"When I walked on to the exit of the swimming pool, the right-left, I could really see Michael was doing something totally different with the car. Really, really, obviously different. But you know, I couldn't really tell you what. I couldn't tell you whether he was understeering or oversteering or how he was braking or what he was doing with the throttle. All I could tell you is that he was different and quicker."

A Ferrari insider later revealed to me that Michael was left-foot braking. But more than that. Because for him, brakes aren't simply a mechanism that slows a car. No. "For Michael, brakes are but one element in an exquisite yet subconscious fusion of techno-dynamic ingredients," said my source.

So as the number 3 Ferrari tore past Damon's baffled gaze that day, inside the cockpit Michael's feet would have been a blur, dancing on the pedals with the agile sensitivity of a Bolivian pickpocket's hands. To be seriously quick these days, my man implied, that's what you've got to be able to do.

Which brings us back to Trulli. A classic karter-turned-racer, Jarno has probably never in his life braked an F1 car with his right foot. Jarno can do the techno-dynamic-fusion bit, too.

Fair enough, you say, but most Fl drivers left-foot brake these days. Indeed they do, but for many it's been a thing they've forced themselves to do. Some never really get the knack. In 1998, for example, Hill's Jordan teammate was Ralf Schumacher—like Trulli, a man who began karting as a small child, a man for whom left-foot braking consequently comes as easy as walking. I asked Jordan's then technical director Gary Anderson why Damon wasn't left-foot-braking. "I think it's a case of: 'I know it's quicker, but I'm 38 and I can't quite get on with it,'" the Irishman replied.

That remark sounds ominously like Rubens Barrichello this year. "Michael brakes with his left foot right into the apex of the corner," Rubens admitted at Monaco, "while I have to take my right foot off the brakes earlier to get back on the power at the same spot as him. I brake with my right foot (for) feel. I've tried using my left foot and it just doesn't feel right. You have to do what you're most comfortable with." Rubens' best lap last Saturday trailed Michael's by a full second, by the way.

Perhaps it's time Rubens put his best foot forward. His left foot. Just ask Damon.

So, according to this theory, if you have not spent a fair amount of time driving a kart by the time you get your drivers license, you will never be a Schumacher or Montoya. While I believe there is a lot of truth in this statement, I certainly don't think that if you haven't grown up driving a kart you should stay away from race car driving. With work, both physically and mentally, you can adequately train your left foot. Of course, the time, focus, and energy spent doing this is time, focus, and energy spent away from working on other areas of your driving. But, it is still well worth it.

So, with all this in mind, why exactly is left-foot braking superior to right-foot braking?

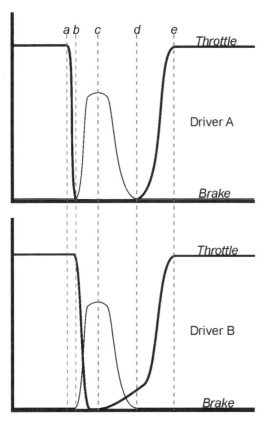

*Compare the throttle-to-brake graph traces from these two drivers at the end of a long straightaway. Driver A is a right-foot braker, while Driver B uses his left foot to brake. As you can see, right-foot braking wastes some time—the amount of time it takes to remove the right foot from the throttle and move it over and onto the brake pedal will cost you (from point "a" to "b" on the graph). With left-foot braking, there is no lost time—the transition from throttle to braking is immediate.*

First of all, left-foot braking allows you to alter the speed of the car—which is what you use the brakes for—without upsetting the balance as much. It is easier to drive smoothly. And any time you can drive smoother, upsetting the balance less, the higher the car's traction limits will be. And that means you can drive faster.

Secondly, it saves time in the transition from throttle to braking to throttle. This is what Barrichello was talking about. With right-foot braking, your right foot must move from the throttle to the brake pedal and back. At the end of a straightaway, that will result in having to brake slightly earlier. In the transition from braking to acceleration, the fraction of a second it takes for your right foot to move from the brake pedal to the throttle is extremely valuable. When using your left foot for braking, that movement or transition doesn't even exist.

In fact, it is possible to actually overlap the end of braking with the beginning of acceleration (squeezing of the throttle) so that there is no time delay at all. If done correctly, the shift in weight balance will be seamless. That saves time and keeps the car better balanced.

With left-foot braking, it is also possible to keep your right foot flat to the floor on the throttle and just alter the speed or balance of the car slightly by braking with the left foot at the same time. This is something that I don't recommend be done a lot, as the brakes will overheat eventually. However, if you need to just get the front of the car to "bite" a bit better at turn-in for a fast, sweeping corner, sometimes a short, quick squeeze of the brake pedal with the left foot while keeping the throttle flat will do the trick. Or, if you need to take just a little bit of speed off, but don't want to lose the engine's momentum, the same left foot brake application may work.

Can a driver be competitive without left-foot braking, using his right foot to brake? Certainly. Dario Franchitti, for example, uses his right foot for braking unless driving on an oval track. In the October/November 1999 issue of *Race Tech* magazine he said, "If the corner requires it, maybe an occasional dab with the left foot, but hardly ever . . . I am left-foot braking here (the Chicago oval) so I don't get that much pedal feel. I can feel when it is about to lock but my left foot certainly isn't as sensitive as my right foot yet. I am more of a traditionalist." Of course, one wonders what Franchitti could do if he had learned to left-foot brake years ago.

## Braking Technique

Okay, okay, you say, that's all very fine for drivers who have cars they can left-foot brake, but my car won't allow it. Many cars, in fact, do not allow left-foot braking. Either it is physically impossible to get your left foot in position, or the gearbox does not allow clutchless shifts. If you are using your left foot for the clutch, you can't use it for the brakes—at least not full time.

You can still learn something from what was just said about the technique, though. The basic advantage of left-foot braking is its ability to make the transition from braking to acceleration as smooth and seamless as possible. Even if you have to use your right foot for braking, that is still your goal.

The speed in which you ease off the brake pedal and the timing of when you come off the brakes as you enter the turns are perhaps the two most important factors in determining the speed you can carry into the corner.

As you know, when you brake to slow the car when approaching a corner, the front of the car dives because weight has transferred onto the front tires. This dive causes the front springs to compress. When you lift your foot off the brake pedal, the springs expand, popping the front of the car up and transferring weight away from the front toward the rear. If you lift your foot off the brake pedal too quickly or abruptly right at the point where you begin to turn the steering into the corner, the front will become unweighted, probably causing it to understeer.

Easing off the brakes slowly (relatively speaking) and gently at just the right speed does three things:

1. It keeps the front of the car loaded (weight transferred onto the front tires), which helps the car turn-in responsively.

2. It often helps you to get back to throttle early and with commitment. As the front is loaded at turn-in, the car will rotate better, which means you will not have to wait or modulate the throttle much. Instead, as the car rotates toward the apex, you will be able to get back on the throttle and stay on it.

3. It does the obvious—as you ease off the brake pedal, you will carry more speed into the corner. And, due to the two points above, the car will be able to handle the extra speed. If you tried to carry that same speed into the corner by coming off the brakes quickly and immediately, the front would become unloaded and the car would most likely understeer—not rotate toward the apex—reducing the car's speed and delaying the point where you could start to accelerate.

Of course, you can ease off the brakes too slowly or gradually. If you ease off the brake pedal too slowly, you will be turning into the corner with too much weight transferred onto the front tires. This may cause the car to oversteer as you turn in. Or, it may cause it to understeer by overloading the front tires. You are asking for more than 100 percent from the front tires, so they give up and begin to slide.

How you ease your foot off the brake pedal dictates the balance of the car and therefore its handling characteristics. Many times, a driver will complain that the car understeers too much just after turn-in, and that it results in him not being able to get back on the throttle early enough. Perhaps all the driver needs to do is ease his foot off the brake pedal a little more slowly.

One's natural conclusion regarding braking on the approach to a corner is to think that braking as late and hard as possible (at the tires' limit) would be ideal and what you should do for each and every corner. But that's not necessarily true. When you approach a corner with the car "standing on its nose" from braking so hard, how well do you think it will grip the track at corner turn-in?

There are some cars and turns where you need to brake lighter, or ask for less than 100 percent from the tires. There are corners that are best approached with the car not standing on its nose. This is something you will need to experiment with. If your car tends to understeer entering a corner, try trail braking more or less to see if either loading the front tires more or less helps. Also, some formula and prototype sports cars are very pitch sensitive—the aerodynamics are negatively affected when the car is too far from being level, or balanced.

The amount you trail brake also plays a role in the line you drive through a corner. The more you trail brake, the earlier you can turn into the corner. The less you trail brake, the later you have to turn in. The reason is that trail braking helps rotate the car for you, so you don't end up running out of track at the exit of the corner. The advantage to turning slightly earlier is that you can carry more speed. The later you turn-in, the sharper you have to turn, meaning you have to be traveling slightly slower. This is what I talked about in Chapter 6.

Obviously, these are general rules and not cast in stone—but they do work most of the time. See the illustration on page 95.

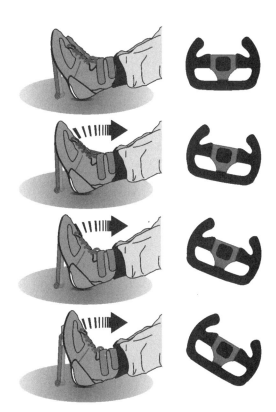

*Trail braking is simply trailing or easing your foot off the brake pedal as you enter the corner. How much you trail brake depends on the car's handling characteristics and the type of turn.*

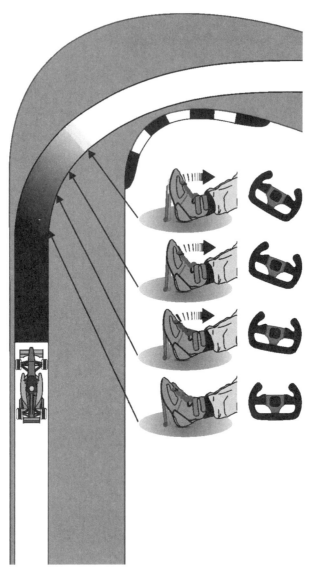

*As you initiate your turn into the corner, slowly and gently ease, or trail, your foot off the brake pedal. This is the only way of ensuring you use up all 100 percent of the tires' traction entering a corner.*

A common error some drivers make is braking too early. That does something other than the obvious of slowing down too soon. If you brake early, you will arrive at the turn-in point feeling like you have slowed the car enough, which you have. The problem is that often this is prior to the turn-in

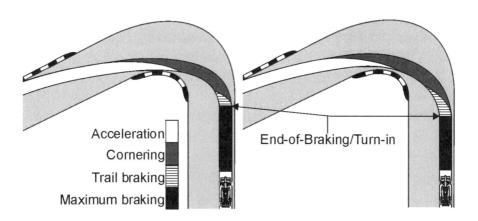

| | |
|---|---|
| Acceleration | |
| Cornering | |
| Trail braking | |
| Maximum braking | |

End-of-Braking/Turn-in

*Trail braking helps "rotate" the car while entering a corner. In general, the more you trail brake, the earlier you can begin turning into a corner (as in the illustration on the right); the less you trail brake, the later and more abruptly you will have to turn in. The later and more abruptly you turn in, the less speed you will be able to carry into the corner.*

point. So, just before turning in, you come off the brakes, unloading the front of the car. As you turn in, the car will not respond the way you would like, either understeering or just feeling unresponsive. The message your brain receives is: we are at the limit. That message, unless recognized, results in you taking the corner at this (slow) speed over and over again, programming it. A lot of drivers do this, particularly when learning a new track or car, and then it becomes a programmed mistake. And I'm not talking about braking way too early—even 5 or 10 feet can cause a huge problem.

It is important to be aware of when you are easing off the brakes. If you begin to release the brake pedal prior to initiating your turn-in, you probably began braking too early.

## Late Braking

When asked what strategy might best be used to improve lap times by three or more tenths of a second on a typical road course, what do you think most race drivers' answer would be? If you guessed, "brake later" you are absolutely right. I know, I've asked many, many drivers this very question.

But is it the best strategy? Start to answer that question by asking yourself the simple question, why do I brake for a corner? The answer is that you have a mental picture or feel for what speed you need to be slowed to by the time you begin to turn in to the corner; you are traveling at "X" speed approaching the corner, and to be slowed to "Y" by the turn-in, you need to begin braking "now" and "this" hard.

In short, you brake to slow the car to a speed you feel is the maximum the car can carry into the turn.

With this in mind, what do you suppose most drivers—and probably you—do when braking later for a corner? Right, you brake later, but harder, for you "know" you need to get the car slowed to "Y" speed by the time you turn in. In fact, until you update your mental picture of your corner entry speed, braking later will only result in you braking harder. Your corner entry speed will be exactly the same. Of course, what often occurs when braking harder is that you lock up the brakes; at best you begin braking a car-length later and enter the corner at the exact same speed as before. The biggest improvement in lap time you will see from this is no more than a few hundredths of a second.

However, if you update your mental picture of the corner entry speed, to "Y + 2 miles per hour," for example, you will naturally brake a little later and not any harder. This will result in carrying more speed into the corner, and you will see tenths of a second improvement in lap time in one single corner.

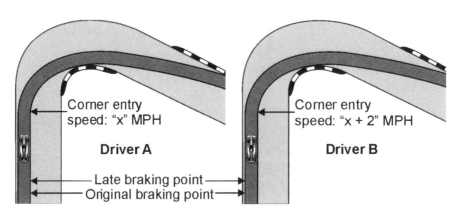

*A comparison of two approaches to going faster. Driver A brakes later, but enters the corner at the same speed as always ("x" miles per hour) by braking harder. Driver B brakes later, but also carries 2 miles per hour more into the turn by braking as hard as usual. Braking later results in a small gain; carrying a little more speed into the turn results in a big gain.*

## Speed Secret #22:
## Corner entry speed is more important than late braking.

This is where the big gains in speed come from. So, instead of simply using the strategy of braking later, change your mental picture of the corner entry speed and you will naturally brake later and carry more speed into the corner.

### Rotation Turns Versus Set Turns

Another factor that determines how much you should trail brake into a corner is whether it is what I call a rotation turn or set turn. Typically, but not always, "rotation turns" are shorter, tighter, slower corners; and "set turns" are longer and faster.

In many fast, sweeping corners, it is best to be on power, on the throttle from the second you turn in. In other words, no trail braking. Why? Because the car is better balanced this way—the car has taken a set. If you enter the turn while trail braking and then transition to acceleration, the car's weight distribution is changing. The weight is transferring off the front and to the rear while the car is cornering. In most cases, a car will have more traction or grip—a higher cornering limit—when it is set, when its weight has stopped transferring from one axle to the other.

This is especially important in corners with a long mid-corner phase. Because you are spending more time in the corner, ultimate cornering grip is critical. In shorter, tighter turns whose mid-corner phase is almost non-existent, the ability to rotate or change the direction of the car is more important than overall cornering grip. In this case, you should trail brake more. Trail braking enables you to rotate or turn and change the direction of the car quicker.

## SPEED SECRET #23:
## The faster and longer the corner, the less trail braking you should use and the earlier you need to be on the power; the slower and tighter the corner, the more trail braking you should use to help rotate the car.

Given the choice, if you could accelerate all the way through every corner, rather than having to slow down and rotate the car, you would do that since the car would have more overall traction. You would be able to maintain a higher speed through the corners. But that is not practical or useable in every corner. The main objective for some corners is to change direction. These are rotation turns, since the main challenge is rotating the car. The main objective in other corners is to maintain as high a speed as possible through the turn. These are set turns.

## Steering Technique

Obviously, the entry phase of a corner requires you to turn the steering wheel to make the car turn. Through the years I've heard numerous discussions and comments on just how a driver should turn the steering. While some people claim you should pull down on the wheel with the hand on the inside of the corner, others say you should push up with the outside hand. The odd thing is, the people handing out these two conflicting pieces of advice are racing and high-performance driving school instructors—supposed experts on the matter. And, both approaches have their pros and cons. Pulling down with one hand usually provides more strength, but may be less sensitive and accurate (less smooth). Pushing up with one hand is more accurate, but takes more effort.

Having heard this argument for years, and trying both methods myself and with drivers I've coached, I think the whole discussion of which hand you should primarily use to turn the steering wheel is a complete waste of time. Driving is a two-handed sport! If you are using just one hand to do most of the work, then you are losing out on both strength and accuracy. While one hand is pushing up, the other hand should be pulling down. While one is pulling down, the other is pushing up. That is where smooth steering inputs come from.

As you approach a corner, there are a number of ways you can turn the steering wheel. You can slowly turn the wheel, or you can quickly crank the wheel. You can start off slowly turning the wheel, and then progressively turn it faster. Or, you can do the opposite, quickly initiating the turn and then progressively turn it slower. You can also turn the wheel a little farther than is required to get the car to go where you want, and then quickly unwind it back out. You can arc or bend the car into a turn, or you can make your turn-in crisp. You can have "slow hands" or "quick hands."

So, which is the right way of turning the steering wheel? I don't think there is a right way. It is all a matter of the type of turn you are approaching, the handling characteristics of your car, and your driving style. It is probably some combination of all the ways I mentioned, and maybe even more.

The point is, some corners require a quick, abrupt turn, and others don't. Some are best when you progressively increase the rate at which you turn the wheel, and others are best suited to the opposite approach. The key, then, is to be able to use whatever approach best suits the particular corner and car. To do that, your driving style must be adaptable. Many drivers have one particular way of turning the steering wheel and cannot adapt their style. That is one of the reasons why some drivers are better in fast corners than they are in slow ones, and vice versa.

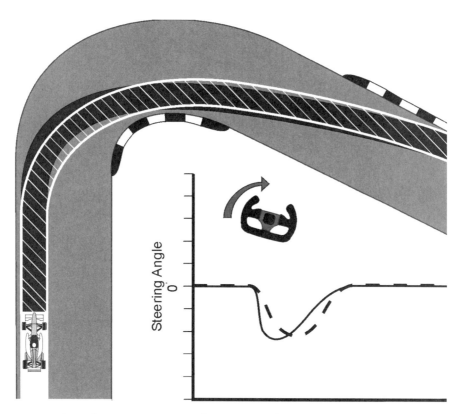

*A comparison of two corner turn-in techniques. One driver eases, or "bends," the car into the corner, while the other driver uses a crisp, abrupt style. Which one is best? It depends on the car and the corner.*

Time for another general rule.

### SPEED SECRET #24:
**The slower the corner, the later the apex, the quicker and crisper you need to turn the steering wheel. The faster the corner, the more you need to arc or bend the car into the turn with slow hands.**

Johnny Herbert, in *Race Tech* magazine (August/September 1999), talked about this very thing and his steering style when entering a corner:

> I have a style which, although it is quite smooth in the corner, has quite a hard turn and with these tires I normally break the grip straight away. So I introduce more understeer than I need in slow corners. Fast corners are no problem, because you have the downforce. The slower you go, the worse it gets. So you have got to be very, very smooth. Last year you could still use the front tire as a brake almost, to scrub off a bit of speed. But with these tires—the extra groove doesn't allow that. It just scrubs and doesn't stop—it just understeers. It breaks the traction of the tire.
>
> It is finding the right thing to do. It is not a natural thing. Naturally I turn in hard. But if you do that you just introduce much more understeer. But it is very easy to say, 'there it is, go and do it'. It is doing it so that it is an advantage. You can't go in slower to stop the understeer, because then you are just too slow anyway. You have to carry the speed or even more speed but be smooth.

The real key to this situation is being aware of how you turn the steering wheel, and then adapting to what works best, not just saying, "this is my style and I'm sticking to it." Of course, this doesn't mean spending all your conscious thought and awareness on what you are doing with the steering wheel as you enter a turn. If you did that, you would most likely end up stuffed into a wall somewhere on the outside of the corner! No, it is simply an overall, relaxed awareness of what you are doing. Usually, by asking yourself some awareness-building questions before, during, and after driving, you will subconsciously become aware of what you are doing. And most important, you will almost certainly turn the steering wheel in the way most suitable for the corner.

The key to steering correctly is to have a solid mental image of what you feel is ideal, and then be aware of what you are doing now. Using MI+A=G, you will automatically (subconsciously, without any conscious thought) and naturally do what is right.

You can, and should, practice becoming aware of how you turn the steering wheel when driving on the street. If you do it enough on the street, it will become a habit, a program when you are on the racetrack. As you turn into a corner, ask yourself, Did I turn the wheel gently and slowly; or did I crank the wheel abruptly? Can I turn the wheel more gently? Did I turn the wheel slowly at turn-in, and progressively turn it faster, or the other way? Did I turn it farther than required to get the car to go where I wanted, and then have to unwind it prior to the apex? Did I unwind the steering from the apex on out and release the car toward the exit?

The more positive questions you ask, and the deeper you dig, the more aware you will become. And that awareness will lead to positive, accurate steering techniques.

Since more and more race drivers today are coming from a karting background, it is important for me to point out one difference between driving some types of karts and race cars. In many karts, one of the techniques used to make the front tires grip and turn in well is to crank the steering wheel in, and then quickly unwind it to the point required to get the kart to follow the desired line. While this works with the particular geometry and lack of suspension on a kart, I can't recommend it for any race car. It is one of the habits (mental programs) that kart drivers have to change when beginning to race cars. If not, they may never reach their full potential racing cars. So, if are you coming into car racing with lots of karting experience, be aware of your steering technique.

## Change in Speed

Okay, enough hinting around. Time to tackle the change of speed problem, one of the most common errors I see drivers make.

The key point is the change in speed through a corner may be causing the car to make you believe you are driving at the limit when, in reality, you have actually created an artificially low limit. Let me use an example to demonstrate what I mean.

Let's assume you can enter Turn 1 of our imaginary track at 80 miles per hour. That is, at the point you initially turn the steering wheel at the turn-in point you are traveling at 80 miles per hour; and, that you can carry or maintain that speed around the apex, where you begin to accelerate. Throughout this corner the car is at its very limit of traction—one-half of 1 mile per hour more and the car would begin to slide too much, causing it to either scrub off speed or start to spin.

Now, what would happen if you entered the corner at less than 80 miles per hour? What often happens is this: You slow the car down to say, 78 miles per hour at the turn-in point. As you enter the corner, your traction sensing tells you that the car is not at the very limit, there is still some traction to be used. So, your right foot pushes down on the throttle pedal and the car accelerates. Understand that this happens entirely at the subconscious level. You are certainly not consciously thinking about doing this, it is just happening.

Although entering the corner at 78 miles per hour is not driving at the limit, it is not far off. The tires are close to being at their limit of traction, just before they break away and begin to slide too much. So, as you begin accelerating, you are now asking the rear tires (in a rear-drive car) to take on a bigger task. Remember, you can only ever get 100 percent out of the tires, nothing more. If you are using 99 percent of the rear tires' traction for cornering at 78 miles per hour, and then begin accelerating, there is a very good chance you will ask for more than 1 percent traction for accelerating. In fact, there is a good chance that with your right foot squeezing down on the throttle, you will be asking for more like 5 or 10 percent of the traction for accelerating. The result is the rear tires go beyond their limit, and the car begins to oversteer, if ever so slightly.

Your read on the situation at this point is that you are driving at or maybe even slightly beyond the limit. And, you are only at somewhere between 78 and 80 miles per hour, which is not as fast as you could be. You think you are at the limit, and you are right to some extent. But, you have created this artificially low limit.

You see, it is the change of speed from 78 to 80 miles per hour that caused the tires to barely exceed the traction limit, and create an artificially low limit. If you had entered the corner at 80 miles per hour, your traction sensing would have told you that you are at the limit, you would have

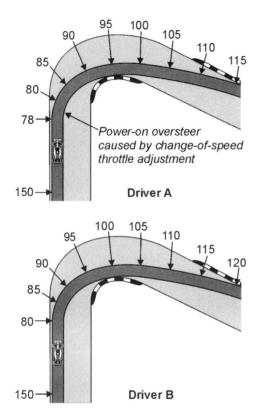

**Driver A**

Power-on oversteer caused by change-of-speed throttle adjustment

**Driver B**

Let's look at Driver A and B again. Both approach the corner at the same speed—150 miles per hour. Driver A slows the car to 78 miles per hour at the turn-in point, turns in and immediately senses that the car is not at the very limit, so he gets on the throttle. This causes a little power-on oversteer, so he eases off slightly to correct before getting back on the throttle, and then increases his speed through the rest of the corner, hitting 115 miles per hour at the exit. Meanwhile, Driver B enters the turn at 80 miles per hour with the car at the limit, then smoothly increases speed throughout the corner, hitting 120 miles per hour at the exit.

squeezed on the throttle appropriately, enabling you to accelerate out of the corner on the limit.

A greater than ideal change in speed also causes excessive weight transfer, and it unbalances the car more than necessary. When your traction sensing signals there is more speed required to get the tires to their limit, you tromp on the throttle and weight is transferred to the rear. Yes, this may be a good thing to help give the rear tires more grip to handle the increased demand for acceleration traction, but it may also cause excessive understeer. The ultimate result is the same: your traction sensing then feels that the front tires are beyond the limit, and you don't go any faster (maybe even slow down).

This is why your corner entry speed is so critical. If you enter a corner too slow (below the limit), and then try to make up for it by accelerating, you may create a limit that is not as high as if you entered the corner at the ideal speed. And, your corner entry speed is one of the reasons your speed sensing skills are so important. Because without great speed sensing skills, you will not be able to accurately and consistently gauge, and therefore drive, the correct speed when entering the turns.

Truly great race car drivers have the ability to adjust their entry speed to within one-half of 1 mile per hour, consistently, of the ideal corner entry speed for every corner and every lap. Lesser drivers' corner entry speed may vary from lap to lap anywhere from 1 to 5 or more miles per hour. Until your speed sensing abilities are finely tuned and consistent, you will never know for sure what technique (or car setup) worked and what didn't work. This is why the speed sensing exercises I presented in Chapter 4 are so critical.

### SPEED SECRET #25:
### The less change in speed through a corner, the faster you will be.

## Downshifting

Not all cars can be left-foot braked, of course, and that dictates how you downshift. If you are right-foot braking, then everything I said in *Speed Secrets* still applies. The key points I made then were:

• Shifting smoothly and precisely is more important than the speed of the shift.

• Use the brakes to slow the car down, and then downshift simply to get the car into the proper gear to accelerate again.

• You will never be a great driver without using the heel and toe downshifting technique (if you are right-foot braking).

Left-foot braking is no excuse for not doing what is equivalent to heel and toe downshifting. In other words, while left-foot braking, your right foot must blip the throttle with each downshift. And that's the case whether you are driving a car with a sequential shift gearbox or not. Anyone who thinks he can get away with just knocking it down a gear without blipping the throttle is really mistaken and will not only be hard on the gearbox but will be slow as well.

Sequential gearboxes are becoming the norm in "real" race cars, and as I said, you must blip the throttle on the downshift. But, with most sequential gearboxes, you should not use the clutch. At this point, some people would then ask, how does that work? With a sequential shifter, the gearbox is always in gear. How can you blip the throttle if it is still in gear?

As you click the shifter forward to downshift, the gearbox does pass through neutral for a fraction of a second. That is when you blip the throttle. Believe me, it is easier to time it right than it sounds. Even as I write this it seems to me that it would be very difficult to time that exactly right. In reality, though, it is as easy as timing your throttle blip with any other type of gearbox. It may take a few laps to get the hang of it, but once you do, it will become a subconscious habit.

## Braking Exercises

Easing off the brakes while coming to a stop when driving your street car teaches your foot the sensitivity and control necessary to ease off the brakes accurately and effectively with the ideal speed and finesse. If you use your left foot for braking on the racetrack, then you need to practice with it on the street. That's easy if you drive an automatic transmission vehicle, and not so easy if you don't.

Even if you drive a manual shift car on the street, you should still practice using your left foot for braking. Any time you approach a corner that does not require downshifting, brake with your left foot. And, although I don't recommend this as a safe street driving tactic, you may want to shift into neutral on the approach to a stop, and then again use your left foot for braking.

Your main objective is to make your braking as smooth as possible. It doesn't have to be hard braking to do that, either. You want to make squeezing on the brakes (very quickly) and easing off of them as natural as breathing.

# Chapter 9

# The Mid-Corner Phase

As I mentioned earlier, the mid-corner phase is what separates the champions from the truly great drivers. At the time of this writing, it seems that only Juan Montoya can come close to Michael Schumacher (Ralf Schumacher is close, but not quite there, and Villeneuve is capable on occasion) in the speed he carries through the middle of each and every turn without it negatively affecting his corner entry and exit speed. In fact, Schumacher's style, technique and ability in the mid-corner phase may even help the other corner phases.

So what exactly does Schumacher do that enables him to carry anywhere from one-half to two miles per hour more through the middle of each corner? Well, I would love to be able to say I know exactly what his "secret" is, but I can't. What I do know is that it has more to do with the way he balances the car than anything else. Although the line he chooses has a little to do with it, that is something that practically every other driver in F1 has figured out, as we have already discussed.

If you ever have the opportunity to really watch Schumacher, you may be able to notice what I'm talking about. If you can stand near the edge of the track, as I've been fortunate enough to do, you can see that the attitude of his car (the pitch and roll) does not change as much as others. His car stays better balanced.

So, again, how does he do it? Without being able to get into the cockpit with him, I can only imagine that his footwork is close to perfect. The way he squeezes on the brakes with his left foot, and then eases off of it while beginning to squeeze the throttle with his right foot, is seamless—perfectly smooth. My guess is that he has the very slightest of overlap between the two—meaning that he has not fully come off the brake before he begins to squeeze the throttle. There certainly does not appear to be

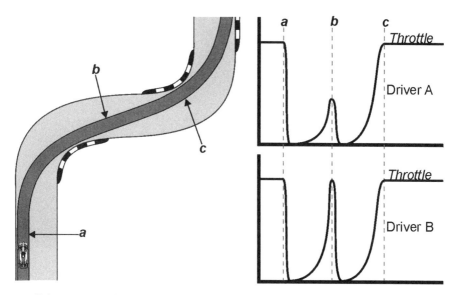

*Small things can make big improvements. For example, compare these throttle graph traces. Between these two turns, Driver A uses less than half throttle, while Driver B gives a short stab at full throttle. Driver B is "hustling" the car. In these Esses, that little burst of throttle could result in being up to three-tenths of a second quicker in this section alone.*

even a nano-second of time where he is not either braking or accelerating. However, I'm sure there is not too much overlap either, otherwise he would be known for being hard on the brakes, which he is not.

Schumacher's mid-corner speed also benefits from his steering technique. He has such light hands on the wheel. It is as if he is hardly gripping it. From the in-car camera, there are times where it looks as though only his fingers are touching the wheel—his palms do not seem to be in contact with the wheel. Of course, to control an F1 car with only fingers holding the wheel would require great physical strength, given the amount of grip and feedback through the steering the car has. Schumacher has a reputation for being perhaps the fittest driver in the world, maybe even in the history of the sport.

This light, sensitive touch that Schumacher has on the wheel does two things. First, it provides him with more feedback from the steering wheel. Any time you grip the steering wheel tightly, tensing the muscles in your arms, the information (vibrations, sense of forces feeding back through the wheel, etc.) from the wheel to your brain will be restricted.

Remember, in Chapter 4 I asked you to try holding the steering wheel of your street car very tightly, and then with a light touch. Which one provided you with the most feedback? The lighter touch, right?

The feedback from the steering wheel provides you with much of your traction sensing. If that is restricted to any degree, you will be less sensitive to how much grip the tires have, and therefore whether you are at the very limit or not.

Michael Schumacher's physical strength may just be one of the keys to his abilities. Due to his strength, his arms and hands may be more relaxed while controlling the steering wheel. Any time you can relax your muscles, the more feedback will reach your brain. The more feedback your brain has, the better your skills will be. And that leads to the second thing that results from the light touch on the steering wheel: smooth, precise, progressive steering inputs.

### SPEED SECRET #26:
### Fast mid-corner speed comes from great entry speed, car balance, and early exit speed.

## Balancing the Car

Having said what makes Schumacher so great, and even though I went to great detail in *Speed Secrets* talking about balancing the car, I want to go over it again.

A car is balanced when there is no weight being transferred forward, as when you are braking; when there is no weight being transferred to the rear, as when you are accelerating; and when there is no lateral weight transfer, as when you are cornering. This is the car's mechanical balance.

Why is a balanced car so important? Because a balanced car has more traction than an imbalanced car, and the more traction the car has, the faster you can drive.

Aerodynamic balance must also be considered. With some cars, the aerodynamic downforce is affected when the car is not balanced—when the car has a nose-dive, rear squat, or roll attitude. In these cars, when the rake of the underside of the chassis changes in relation to the track, the distribution of front to rear downforce can change dramatically. It can also reduce overall downforce. Once again, the better the car's balance, the more traction it has, and the faster you can drive.

So how do you balance the car better than your competitors? Well, that has to do with using the controls smoothly, not doing anything too abruptly to upset the balance, and then having a great sense of personal balance to become aware of the car's balance. Your footwork, for example, is critical. Without smooth, quick, and seamless transitions from throttle to brake, and brake to throttle, the car's balance will suffer.

A great personal sense of balance may be the final reason Schumacher has the ability to carry so much speed through the mid-corner phase. He has an amazing sense of balance, not just his own personal balance, but the car's balance.

*Driving at the limit requires keeping the car as balanced as possible—as if it were balancing on top of a single point.*

Balancing the car in a way that allows maximum mid-corner speed also has much to do with the braking technique used when approaching and entering the turns. Why? If you brake very hard, standing the car on its nose during the entry to a corner, the car's balance will not be ideal for the rest of the corner. If you can brake hard on the approach, while being able to re-balance the car as you ease off the brakes during the entry phase, your mid-corner speed will be good—without having to be too slow on the approach.

Before you begin to think I consider Michael Schumacher to be some kind of superhero, understand that there are other drivers who are very good at this as well. Alex Zanardi, for example, was extremely good at this when racing CART Champ cars, although he had a difficult time with it in F1. Motorsport journalist Jonathan Ingram made the perfect observation in his "Inside Line" column published in *On Track* (February 17, 2000):

> It seems the transition from Champ cars to both grooved tires and carbon brakes must have been a major problem. Zanardi's speed in CART came from not just braking late with cast iron equipment, but *braking more lightly entering the corners* [italics added]. That's why his moves seemed so unusual to fans, stewards and fellow drivers—he often *carried unexpected speed in the middle of the corners.* With less tire on the road and carbon brakes that needed to be leaned on heavily to bring them up to operating temperature, Zanardi's American success could not be translated.

By the way, I don't believe his struggles in F1 had anything to do with him losing his skills or technique. It was that he could not access them as well. Why? I believe it had more to do with his comfort level within the team, and his lack of ability to adapt his behavioral traits to suit the environment within that team. Had he been comfortable in his surroundings, he would have carried the same type of speed in the Williams F1 car that he did in Champ cars.

*In some cars, running your inside tires over the curbing can help load the outside tires, providing them with more grip. Of course, this depends on the size and shape of the curb. In addition, running over the curb usually straightens out the corner, increasing its radius.*

## Transition

If you cannot make the transition from brake to throttle in the corner seamlessly, you will never carry good mid-corner speed. This is another area where left-foot braking has an advantage, as it is much easier to make a seamless transition. In fact, when using your left foot on the brake and right on the throttle, there is usually a little bit of overlap, making it much smoother.

A seamless transition from the brakes to the throttle results in a balanced car and fast mid-corner speed.

Practice your throttle-brake-throttle transition until you can do it in such a way that if someone were to ride with you blindfolded, they would not be able to tell the exact point where the braking ended and where the acceleration began. That is what I mean by a seamless transition. If you are right-foot braking, the movement of your foot off the brake pedal and onto the throttle should be practiced on the street until it is perfectly smooth.

# Chapter 10

# The Unknown Corner

How do I estimate the speed and braking through a corner I have never been through before? There's a question every rally and autocross driver would love the "secret" answer to. Even road and oval track racers could use it, although it is not as important since they have the advantage of being able to go around and around until they figure it out using trial and error. So, let's take a look at what you're up against when faced with a corner you've never been through before, and see what we can do to discover that "secret."

Approaching an unknown corner, there are four interrelated factors that come into play:

**Speed Sensing:** Your ability to sense, determine, and establish a particular speed. Obviously, this must be done at an intuitive level, not by looking at the speedometer.

**Traction Sensing:** Your ability to feel or sense whether and how close your tires are to their limit.

**Database:** You have a database of information from the hundreds, thousands, or millions of corners you've driven in your life. Your database is primarily made up of visual images of what corners look like, along with the resulting speed and traction sensing information. If your speed sensing and traction sensing skills are poor (a lack of sensory input), the database will not be accurate or as useful as it could be. Of course, you could say your database is just experience—seat time—and you would be right to some extent. But why, then, do some drivers with little experience seem to have a larger database? The better your speed sensing and traction tensing (sensory input), the better (richer) your database will be. In other words, your database is made up of tens, hundreds, thousands, or millions of reference points—those you see, those you feel, and those you hear. It's as if the file of information on each corner is much thicker or deeper with the greater amount of sensory information you have taken in.

**Car Control:** Car control is your ability to "dance" with the car, handling the controls in such a way as to keep the car on your desired cornering line, while keeping the tires at or near their limit.

So, heading into a corner, your speed sensing skills sense the speed (obviously) you're traveling at that instant, and your traction sensing says "we are *this* close to the limit." All the while your database compares the visual image of the corner with others in its files, recalls one that most closely matches, and makes the best estimate of the speed required. Then, it relies on your speed sensing skills to manage the adjusting of speed (slowing down) to *that* speed. At that point your traction sensing skills begin to take over, sensing "how close to the limit" you are. That is when your car control skills come in. If the speed estimate is too high, or your speed sensing didn't do a good job of matching the estimate, then you have to control and manage the extra speed as best you can. Of course, if the estimate was too low, or your speed sensing over-slowed you, then your car control skills will have to do what it takes to increase your speed.

Once you've driven the corner once, it is added to your database. Once it's in the database, you can begin to work with it using mental imagery. Using the information in your database, along with Awareness, you can update the database without necessarily driving. Ask yourself, "How close to the limit was I? If I carried 1 mile per hour more into the

*Approaching a turn you've never seen before, like one on an autocross or slalom course, your mind goes through an amazing process to determine at what speed to which you should slow. It begins by comparing a visual picture of the turn with all of the ones stored in your brain's database.*

corner, what would happen? Two miles per hour more? Three miles per hour more?" Close your eyes, relax, and picture a mental image of that speed. But do more than just visualize it. Include more than just visual information. Also imagine how it feels and what it sounds like. That is true mental imagery, mental programming.

Then, the next time out, simply compare the two, your mental image with your awareness of how close you are to that mental image of the ideal speed. This is using MI + A = G—the simplest, quickest and most effective way that I know to learn and improve. The stronger and more vivid your mental image, and the more awareness you have, the more effective this will be and the easier it is to achieve your goal.

If I had to simplify all of what I just said into "the secret" it would be the following: Work at improving your speed sensing and traction sensing by practicing taking in more sensory input from your vision, your kinesthetic sense (balance, feel, touch, g-forces, vibrations, pitch and roll of the car, etc.), and your hearing.

Practice listening to the car. What is the engine note saying? What are the sounds coming from the tires telling you? Does the tire noise continue to get louder and louder, or does it taper off after the tires reach their limit? Are they growling, howling, squealing, screeching, or screaming? What does that tell you about their grip levels?

Practice feeling the dynamics of the car. Does the steering get heavier or lighter as the tires reach their limit? How much body roll is there before the tires begin to lose their grip? Remember, the tires are talking to you. Are you listening?

Practice seeing more. Take in more visual information. Act like a sponge, soak up sensory information. Then, simply be aware. If you combine awareness—sensory input—with a mental image of what you want to achieve, you will reach your goal of driving at or near the limit, even if it is the first time you've driven through the corner.

And that's the "secret" to knowing what speed to enter a corner you've never seen before. Use your database, your speed sensing, your traction sensing, and then your awareness as you do it so that you can add that to your mental image later. Of course, that adds to your database, and the whole cycle continues, getting better and better each and every time you drive. And that is the secret: improving every time out.

## SPEED SECRET #27:
### *Sensory input and awareness are the keys to driving fast, no matter how the corners appear.*

For those of you who thought I was going to provide you with a secret such as "always slow down 2 miles per hour for each foot of turn radius," and "always turn in 6.73 feet before the pylon," I apologize. It's just not that simple (like you didn't already know that!).

If you look at every run, every stage, or every lap from this perspective, and you are soaking up information to add to your database, my bet is that you will be immediately quicker. There are two reasons for this. First, when you give your brain more information to work with, it will produce a better result. And second, with this approach it is more likely that you will relax and drive more at the subconscious level rather than "trying" to go fast.

# Chapter 11

# *Adaptability*

One of the key areas that separates good race drivers from great race drivers is the ability to adapt their driving to suit the car's handling, to adapt from one type of car to another.

Some drivers, despite how the car is handling, will only drive it one way—their style. And guess what? A driver's style will never suit every handling characteristic. If you cannot adapt your style to suit the car's handling, a change in track conditions, a mechanical problem, or a different type of car, I doubt you will ever be a real champion race driver.

In 1994, Michael Schumacher finished second in the Spanish Grand Prix, despite the fact his Benetton was stuck in fifth gear. What was really impressive was that other than for about two laps when he first encountered the problem (as he figured out how to adapt his driving to the situation), no one but his team even realized he had a problem. His lap times barely changed. That is one of the reasons he is the champion that he is.

Although it would be impossible to list every possible problem scenario you may someday face when racing, I am going to attempt to identify the most common ones and give you some suggestions as to what you may be able to do to adapt your driving to help the situation.

The overall objective with the following suggestions is to give you some knowledge to what you may be able to do to reduce the effect of the problem. In other words, what can be done so the problem has the least effect on your lap times and your ability to race your competitors? Of course, if at all possible, you would adjust the car: the anti-roll bars, brake bias, weight jacker, etc. But if you don't have any more adjustment, or any adjustment to begin with, it is all up to your adaptability once you are in the race.

As I said, being able to jump from one type of car to another is also an important element to being a great race driver. For example, having the skill and knowledge to be able to drive, a rear-wheel-drive, purpose-built race car running on slicks and a front-wheel-drive, production-based car running street tires will greatly increase your chances of being a hired gun. Therefore, I will also try to cover the basics of the differences in driving style required for different types of cars.

### SPEED SECRET #28:
### Improve your adaptability through knowledge and practice.

Of course, I'm giving you this information or knowledge at the conscious level. For you to truly use it, you will need to make it a part of your subconscious by programming it using mental imagery. Until it becomes a subconscious program, the information will be next to useless and you will not be able to access it efficiently while at speed and under racing conditions.

## Corner Entry Understeer
The best place to start when trying to figure out what you can do with your driving technique to help any handling problem is to think about the weight balance of the car. If your car is understeering in the entry portion of a corner, consider what you can do to induce some forward weight transfer; and, what you can do to lessen the weight transfer to the rear.

To increase the forward weight transfer, you can increase or lengthen the amount of time spent trail braking into the corner. That means not trailing, or easing off, the brake pedal so quickly, keeping a little more pressure on the pedal for a little longer. And, if it is a corner that requires

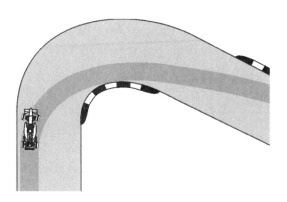

*Corner entry understeer.*

little to no trail braking, then it may be a matter of waiting a little longer—being more patient—before beginning to accelerate; or, squeezing on the throttle a bit more gently.

One of the challenges is when you are chasing another car. As you approach and enter the corners, the distance between your car and the competitor's car is reduced. Visually, it seems you are catching him (even if the time gap has not changed—it is just that you are traveling at a slower speed). So, your natural instinct in trying to catch him is to actually ease off the brakes and get back to throttle a little sooner. That, of course, exaggerates the understeer, slowing you a little more. Then, you *try* a little harder, carrying more speed into the corner, causing more understeer, overheating the front tires more, causing more understeer, you *try* even more . . . and so on. As you can see, the problem just gets worse and worse.

The key, then, is to be patient. You will probably end up entering the corner 1 mile-per-hour or so less. If you focus on increasing the forward weight transfer, and decreasing the rear weight transfer, you will be able to get the car rotated (turned) earlier in the corner and get back to throttle solidly without having to come back off it to control the understeer. That will improve your acceleration out of the corner and down the straight, giving you a better chance at passing the opposition.

Avoid the temptation to turn in a little earlier. If anything, you want to turn in a little later, opening up the exit line so that you can focus on the acceleration phase of the corner.

One of the benefits to trail braking more is that you may actually be able to begin your braking slightly later (since you are doing more of the slowing down in the entry phase). However, that may also be part of the cause of the understeer problem—overloading the front tires. If you are carrying lots of speed into the corner, still have a fair amount of braking going on, and trying to get the front tires to change the direction of the car, you may be asking too much from them. In this case, the cure is to begin braking a little sooner and trail brake a little less. Be patient.

If the weight balance of the car is not the cause or the cure of the understeer, then you have to consider one other thing. It doesn't matter where in the corner the understeer is—think about what you are doing with the steering wheel. Often times, corner entry understeer is caused by the driver cranking in too much steering input, or cranking it in too abruptly. Try turning the steering wheel a little less and a little more gently. I know it may not feel right: The car is not turning enough (understeering), so you turn the steering less? Exactly. Keep the front tires at an angle that they can work at. If you steer the front tires too much, they can't help but give up their grip and begin to slide.

Again, be aware of how much steering you have input, and try taking some out. Or, turn the steering wheel a little slower, a little more gently as you initiate your turn-in. Give the tires a chance to build up their cornering grip.

## Corner Entry Oversteer

Oversteer is often a result of too much weight on the front tires, and not enough on the rears. If that is the case during the entry phase of a corner, that probably means you are braking too hard into the corner and you are trail braking too much.

The cure then is pretty simple. Just begin braking slightly earlier and trail off the brakes a little sooner as you enter the corner. Perhaps, especially if it is a corner that requires little to no braking, it is a matter of beginning to accelerate sooner (but very gently), transferring more weight onto the rear tires.

Again, when you are chasing another competitor, it is easy to fall prey to the "brake late and I catch him" impression. Always keep in mind that you will gain more, both on your competitors and in reducing your lap times, by early acceleration than you will by late braking.

One other thing that may help reduce corner entry oversteer is to turn the steering wheel less abruptly. Ask the car to change directions from straight forward to a curved path a little more progressively.

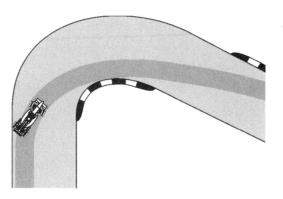

*Corner entry oversteer.*

## Mid-Corner Understeer

Usually the best way to handle mid-corner understeer is simply by smoothly modulating the throttle to change the weight balance of the car. In other words, just breathe (gently lift off) the throttle to cause some forward weight transfer, giving the front tires more grip.

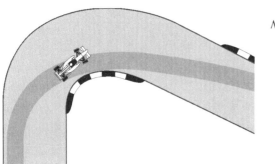

*Mid-corner understeer.*

Often, the understeer is not related to the car's setup, but you have gotten back on the throttle to begin accelerating just a little too abruptly or early. Again, just breathe the throttle to transfer some weight forward.

Also, just like with the entry understeer, be aware of the amount of steering input you have dialed in. Perhaps the cure to your car's mid-corner understeer problem is just unwinding the steering a little bit to allow the front tires to get some grip.

## Mid-Corner Oversteer

Dealing with a mid-corner oversteer is almost always done by changing the car's weight balance. In this case, that means squeezing more throttle on. However, one of the reasons the car has begun to oversteer is that the speed you are carrying is slightly more than the rear tires can handle. So, the last thing in the world you need right then is a bunch more speed. That is why it is critical to squeeze on just a little more throttle.

The mid-corner oversteer could also be caused by wheelspin (in a rear-wheel-drive car, of course), which should be dealt with by being a little easier on the throttle.

If your car's setup is the cause of the wheelspin, about all you can do is be as gentle as possible with the acceleration, and possibly alter your line slightly. If possible, try driving the car a little deeper into the corner

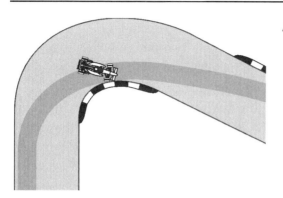

*Mid-corner oversteer.*

before turning in, make the initial turn radius a bit sharper, aim for a later apex, and then let the steering unwind as early as possible. This makes for a straighter acceleration line, meaning that there will be less cornering force to combine with the acceleration force that you are asking from the rear tires.

## Exit Understeer

If your car has an exit understeer problem, the best thing you can do without reducing your acceleration is to alter your line. Your prime objective is to lessen the amount of time you are turning the car while accelerating. So, if you turn in a little later and sharper (even if this means slowing the car down a little) and aim for a later apex, it will allow you to unwind the steering a bit earlier. That means you will be accelerating in a straighter line, reducing the harmful effects of the understeer.

And one more thing. The more gentle you are with the acceleration, the less understeer you will have. If you jump on the throttle, the understeer is going to be exaggerated. So, squeeze on the throttle.

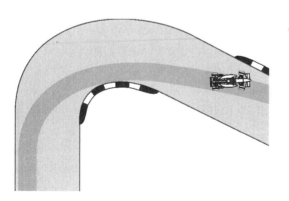

*Corner exit understeer.*

## Exit Oversteer

Exit oversteer can be related to one of two things: either it is power oversteer, caused more by the car's inability to put its acceleration traction to the ground; or it is due to the weight balance.

Usually, the way to deal with either type of exit oversteer is much the same as with exit understeer. The goal is to open up the exit of the corner, increasing the radius of the corner as soon as possible, by using a later turn-in and exit.

One of the other things you have to keep in mind with exit oversteer is to be gentle with the throttle under acceleration. If you stand on the throttle, even if you have altered your line, you are going put a big load on the rear tires. In time, this will overheat them, making the oversteer problem worse, even causing it to oversteer in other parts of the corner.

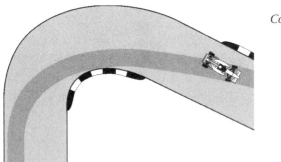

*Corner exit oversteer.*

There is one other approach to dealing with a car that oversteers at the exit of a corner—especially one that has an extreme oversteer problem—and that is to almost give up, or sacrifice, that part of the corner. Instead of slowing the car down and using a later turn-in and apex, you pretty much do the opposite. As you approach the corner, you brake later and carry much more speed into the corner, taking an earlier apex, and then get the car straightened out and pointed down the straight well after the apex. The idea here is that since the car will not accelerate out of the corner very well, you might as well try to take advantage of where the car is working—the corner entry.

Before using this technique, I would make sure that every other technique didn't work, because you will not be setting any track records using this approach. It is a bit extreme! However, once in a race, it may help you to hold off a competitor behind you, at least for a few laps. Perhaps the biggest challenge in using this technique is that it is unlikely you have a mental program for it. Therefore, you may just want to try it on a test day or during a practice session sometime, so that you are prepared for it.

## Oval Track Technique

Everything I just said applies equally to road course and oval tracks. However, there are a couple of things you must keep in mind when driving on an oval. The first and foremost is, if the car is not handling well, do not try to force it to go fast. If you try to make a bad handling car go fast on an oval, at best you will spin. At worst you will end up in the hospital. This is especially the case with an oversteering car.

Oval tracks are not very forgiving, and a bad-handling car can get you hurt. You need to decide whether to continue or not with a bad-handling car. You won't get any more credit for driving a car with evil handling to a mediocre finishing position than you will for bringing it in to make adjustments to it. You will get a lot less credit for stuffing the car into a wall than you will for making a smart decision.

Remember, it is your car's life, and sometimes your own life, on the line. It's your decision.

If your car is oversteering on the oval and you choose to continue, you need to have very smooth, gentle hands. In other words, don't turn the steering any more than you have to and let the steering unwind as soon and as much as possible. With an oversteering car, a natural reaction is to hold the car away from the wall at the exit of the corners. And that is about the very worst thing you can do. The more you hold it away from the wall, the more likely it is that you will hit it!

Also, with an oversteering car, make your initial turn-in as gentle and progressive as possible. Do not make an abrupt turn-in.

With an understeering car on an oval, turn the steering even less—perhaps by driving a higher line through the turns. Let the car run free and release it from the turns.

When adapting to understeer, use the same weight balance adjustment techniques I suggested above, while becoming very aware of what you are doing with the steering. As the car pushes, it will be instinctual to turn the steering a little more. As you know, this is not a good thing. Typically what happens is eventually the front tires scrub off enough speed that they begin to grip again, but now you have so much steering input dialed in that the rear end breaks loose and the car spins. It is amazing how often a spin that appears to be caused by oversteer is actually the result of understeer.

## Brake Fade

Brake fade is one of the scariest things a race driver ever experiences. But unless you want to just give up and pull into the pits every time it happens, you are going to have to live with it at some point in your career.

Typically, there are two reasons for the brakes to fade, both having to do with overheating. The first and most common is when the brakes get so hot from the repeated use that the brake fluid in the system begins to boil. As it boils, air bubbles are created. Unfortunately, air is much easier to compress than brake fluid, so your brake pedal becomes soft and spongy, sometimes to the point that the pedal travels all the way to the floor without applying much pressure to the brake pads.

The second reason for brake fade has to do with the overheating of the pads themselves. In this case, the temperature of the pads has risen to a point beyond their designed operating range. When that happens, a gas is actually boiled out of the pad material, but it doesn't just float away. It forms a layer between the pad and the brake rotor surface, acting almost like a lubricant. With this situation, the brake pedal stays nice and firm no matter how hard you push on it, but the car just doesn't slow down very well.

In either case, the problem you have to deal with is the overheating of the brake system. The only thing you can do is allow the brakes to cool down, which is not an easy thing to do when trying to drive at the limit. In reality, there is no way you can drive at the limit, at maximum speed, while cooling the brake system. There are, however, some ways that you can allow the brakes to cool somewhat without it affecting your speed too much.

As I've talked about previously in this book and my other ones, braking later for corners does not gain you very much. There is much more to be gained when accelerating than there is when braking. Therefore, braking a little bit earlier will not hurt your lap times that much, as long as you brake lightly so that your corner entry speed is just as high as it was before. And braking lightly means less heat going into the brake system.

The overall goal, actually, is to put as little heat into the system, while letting it cool as much as possible by allowing air to flow through them.

If there are any places on the racetrack where you now come off the throttle and brake for a very short period of time, this is an opportunity to help the brakes cool. Instead of touching the brakes, just come off the throttle a little more, or longer. Even if you had been using the brakes for even a fraction of a second, by not using them here you allow the air to cool them without adding any more heat to them.

## Ailing Gearbox

The first thing to consider is why the gearbox is beginning to fail. Is it because you are not blipping the throttle enough on your downshifts (probably beating up on the dog rings)? Are you lifting on your upshifts? Have you missed one shift, damaging the dog ring, and now it pops out of that gear?

If you are driving a car with a sequential shift, there is not much you can do about how you place the gearbox in gear. It is just a matter of pulling backward or pushing forward all the way and being firm and positive with it. But, you can control the use of the throttle. On upshifts, make sure that you exaggerate the throttle lift, which takes the load off the dog rings prior to moving to the next gear. And on downshifts, make sure you are blipping the throttle enough.

If you do not have a sequential shift gearbox, there are a couple of other things you can do, aside from careful use of the throttle on upshifts and downshifts (which applies here as well). The first, and most obvious, is to make sure you do not miss any gear changes, even if that means shifting slower and more deliberately. But just as I said with a sequential shifter, be firm and positive with your shifts. Just as many gearbox failures have occurred by "babying it" as from being too rough.

With a troublesome non-sequential gearbox, you can work at "placing" it in gear a little more. Be precise, but firm and positive. If it begins to pop out of gear, that means the gearbox dog rings have worn. About all you can do is make sure you do not miss any more shifts, and try holding it in the gear that is having the problem.

Whether you use the clutch or not to shift is an important factor. If you do not use the clutch and the gearbox begins to get difficult to shift, won't go into a gear, or pops out of gear, you may want to try using it. If you have been left-foot braking and now need to change to right-foot braking to allow your left foot to work the clutch, that will be quite a change. If you do not have the mental program to drive that way, it may be a bit too much of a change to make in the middle of a race. It may be something you want to try in a practice or test session someday.

If you are driving a car with a synchromesh transmission, like a production-based car, you may want to try double-clutching if it begins to get difficult to get it into gear. If you do not know how to double-clutch, please read *Speed Secrets*.

## Different Cars, Different Techniques

In *Speed Secrets,* I stated that every technique used to drive a rear-wheel drive car applies to driving any other car, whether it is a front-wheel drive or all-wheel drive. That is still accurate. However, there is one rather subtle but important thing you should keep in mind when switching from one type of car to another. Fortunately, it can be summed up in one statement.

### SPEED SECRET #29:
### The higher a car's moment of inertia, the earlier and more gently you need to turn in.

What does this mean? Imagine holding a 4-foot-long barbell with a 10-pound weight at each end above your head with one hand. If you twist or rotate the barbell in one direction and then back in the other direction, what happens? It would be difficult to change direction, causing your arm to twist prior to stopping rotation in one direction and going back in the other.

Now imagine sliding those two 10-pound weights towards the center of the barbell, until they are about an inch from either side of your hand. Rotate or twist the bar again and then reverse direction. It's much easier to change direction, right?

The same thing occurs with a car. The further the mass or weight of the car is distributed from the center of the car (as with a production car), the higher its moment of inertia, and the more difficult it will be to change its direction. The closer the mass of the car is located to the center (as with an open-wheel car), the quicker responding and more maneuverable it will be.

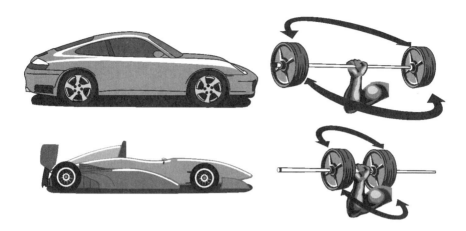

*A vehicle's "polar moment of inertia" can be compared to a barbell. The more a car's weight is concentrated toward its center, the easier and quicker it will respond to a change in direction. You need to adapt your driving technique to suit your car's polar moment of inertia, by changing—amongst many things—the timing and motion of your initial turn-in. Usually, the higher your car's polar moment of inertia, the sooner you need to begin turning in as it will take longer to respond.*

Therefore, when driving a car with a high moment of inertia, it will take longer for it to react to your initial turn-in. To compensate, begin your turn-in slightly earlier and make the turn of the steering wheel more progressive. If you don't do that, you will probably find yourself struggling to get the car tucked right in close against the apex without over-slowing the car.

# Chapter 12

# *Managing Errors*

If I were to ask you what the differences are between an experienced, winning race driver and a less experienced driver, one of your responses would probably be that the former makes fewer errors. I disagree. From my own experience and observations, experienced drivers do not make any fewer mistakes than inexperienced ones. The difference is that the experienced driver recognizes his error sooner, and then minimizes the effects of it.

How does this happen? Why is the experienced driver able to recognize and minimize the effects of errors better? The answers to these questions have to do with a driver's sensory input and the amount of reference points he has. Let me explain.

How many reference points do you have for your favorite corner? Drivers who appear to make a lot of errors (often inexperienced ones) usually have four basic reference points at most (braking point, turn-in, apex, and exit), plus maybe one or two others (e.g. left front tire should pass over the seam in the pavement, straddle the concrete patch, etc.). Experienced drivers literally have thousands in each and every turn. That is why it appears as though they rarely makes errors.

Let's look at an example. As an inexperienced driver turns into a corner too early, he may not recognize the problem until he gets to the apex. The reason is, of course, because beyond the turn-in point, his next reference point to compare his progress to is the apex. As anyone who has turned into a corner too early knows, if you turn in early and don't make a correction or adjustment, you are going to drive off the track at the exit. If you have to make the correction or adjustment at the apex (probably easing off the throttle and turning the steering a little more—often a dangerous combination!), it is most likely going to have to be a fairly large one.

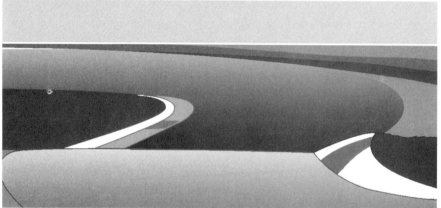

*The more reference points—the more sensory input—you have, the earlier and more subtle your error corrections will be. When faced with the same section of track, two drivers may not perceive or pick up the same amount of references. Notice how much more information the driver in the upper scene is taking in than the driver in the bottom scene.*

Instead, if you have some type of reference 3 feet past the turn-in point and recognize that you are not matching it, your correction or adjustment is going to be much more subtle. In fact, someone observing may never even notice that you made an error or correction.

So, the more reference points you have around a track, the less errors you will appear to make. In fact, you may not even notice the errors yourself; you seem to correct them before they even occur.

This also applies to decision making. If you are making a financial investment, are you more likely to make the right decision if you have more information? Absolutely. The same thing applies to racing wheel-to-wheel. If you are heading into a turn in a pack of cars, the more information you have, the better your passing decisions are going to be. There are top-level pro drivers who have reputations for making bad decisions, all because they are lacking some little piece of information. For some reason, they are missing some sensory input.

I should mention that just because a driver has more experience doesn't automatically mean that he has more reference points, and, therefore is better at minimizing the effects of his errors; or that inexperienced drivers have fewer reference points. Think of it more like a trend: As a driver gains experience, he usually gets better at absorbing information to input into his brain/computer. But, believe me, that is not always the case. I have seen some novices who are better at taking in information than other drivers who have been at it for 20 years.

### SPEED SECRET #30:
### The more reference points you have, the fewer errors you will appear to make.

Let's try to tie all this altogether. Where and how does a driver acquire more reference points? Is it only through more experience, more seat time? Well, that usually helps. But, a driver can speed up the process. How? Simply by focusing on it. By practicing being more sensitive. By increasing the quality and quantity of sensory input.

Of course, I'm talking once again about doing Sensory Input Sessions. Most drivers have never done these. Those that have often end up with a reputation for being very fast, not making mistakes, and being great test drivers because of their sensitive and accurate feedback on what the car is doing. Those that don't do these . . . well, you know what their reputation is.

Let's go back to the most common—the classic—error made by race drivers: apexing a corner too early. This is caused by either turning in too early or too abruptly. In either case, the ultimate result is a line that ends up with your car running out of track at the exit point and either dropping wheels off the outside of the track, spinning back across the track (when the driver makes a last second correction by turning the steering wheel more), or hitting the wall. That is, unless you make a correction in the

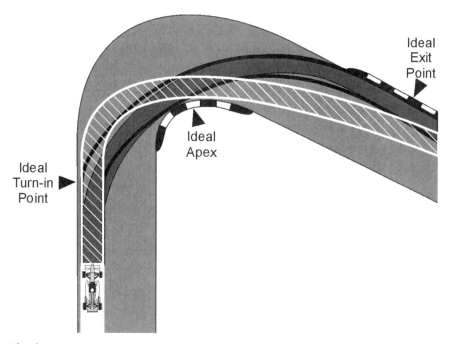

*The three most common errors made at turn-in: turning in too late (the white striped line), turning in too early (the solid shaded line), and turning in too abruptly from the right spot. The keys to eliminating or minimizing these errors are to have a strong mental image of the turn-in point and the turn-in steering motion, as well as looking around the corner and not just through it.*

middle of a corner, which shouldn't be too difficult if you recognize the problem early enough.

The problem is that some drivers—way more than I think should ever do this—either do not recognize the error soon enough or don't know how to correct it. Which is surprising, considering how easy it is to do both.

If your car is against the inside of the corner before the apex, you have made an error and have apexed early. The cure is simple: An adjustment in speed and/or steering is all that is required. If you are normally at full throttle and unwinding the steering wheel at the apex, then you are going to have to ease up on the throttle slightly (a big lift is probably going to make the car spin) and hold or tighten the radius until you get back on your normal, ideal line.

Of course, this assumes that you know exactly where the apex of the corner is. If not, then you had better get a well-defined and recognizable apex reference point. If you don't already have one for every corner on the track, that may be the root cause of an early turn-in. In this case, it is a matter of not knowing exactly where you are going. The old saying, "You're never going to get somewhere if you don't know where it is you're going," certainly applies to this situation.

Again, this is why having as many easily recognizable reference points as possible is so critical. And that comes from focusing on absorbing them through your senses during practice.

### SPEED SECRET #31:
### Minimize errors through maximizing sensory input.

One of the most frustrating things I see race drivers do is assume that if something doesn't work once, it will never work. It's a very common "error."

Let's say you think that you can carry a bit more speed—1 or 2 miles per hour more—into Turn 6 and still get great acceleration out of the corner. You know this will make a significant improvement in your lap times. You head out onto the track, and after a couple of laps you carry a bit more speed into the turn, the car understeers a little wide, and you can't get the car down to the apex. Your conclusion is that the car cannot handle that little bit more speed, and you go back to your original corner entry speed.

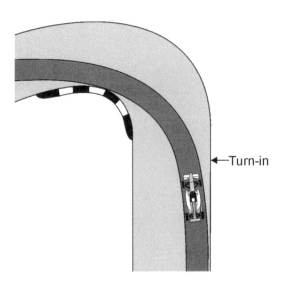

←Turn-in

*A common error that many drivers make is "crabbing" into the corner—easing the car away from the very edge of the track prior to turning in. That's cheating—and it's going to cost you. Be aware if your car is right against the track edge at your turn-in point.*

Sound familiar? I bet it does. And no, this conclusion is not made at the conscious level, but at the subconscious level. You may not even be aware it is happening, but your sense of self-preservation will automatically adjust your speed back to the original "I won't crash at this speed" corner entry.

In many cases, the problem is not the added speed, but rather a lack of technique adjustment to go along with the speed. In this case, perhaps if you had trail braked a little more as you carried more speed into the turn, the car may have rotated toward the apex very nicely, and you would have been much quicker. In fact, some times when a driver works to carry more speed into a corner, he simply eases off the brakes earlier—he trail brakes less. Yes, that will result in more corner entry speed, but without the ideal amount of trail braking, the car may not handle it.

It may be a case of blaming the wrong "cause."

So, just because you can't make a small increase in speed seem to work, don't discount it entirely. Re-think how you approach that section of the track. Maybe by altering your technique slightly you can make the car stick *with* the added speed.

Remember the four stages from Chapter 5: the line, corner exit, corner entry, and mid-corner. As your corner entry speed increases, you may need to alter your line, for example.

### SPEED SECRET #32:
### *Just because a change doesn't work the first time, re-think and try it again. Alter your technique to make the increase in speed work.*

You see, it is not a matter of making less errors, it is simply managing them. Once you realize this, you will undoubtedly make fewer of them. Why? Because, in most cases, you will stop trying to avoid making them. Trying not to make an error is a sure-fire way of ensuring you make them. When you buy into the idea that your job is simply to minimize the effects of errors, life gets much easier.

# Chapter 13

# Case Studies

My goal for this book is to help you continually improve as a race driver. I wish it was practical for me or someone else to coach you each and every time you went on the track. Wow, would you see improvement no matter what level you are at right now! Unfortunately, that's not practical. What is practical is for you to coach yourself. This chapter's objective is to help you do that by providing some examples of how drivers improve.

Whenever I coach a driver, I write up pre-race or test objectives, followed by a post-race or test report that reviews what the driver learned, what needs to be worked on in the future, and a general assessment of the session. I've often looked back at some of these reports and thought, "What a great learning tool for other drivers." And yet, to respect the drivers' privacy, I won't let anyone else see these reports. Still, I thought the information contained in them was too valuable to not share.

So, I want you to meet a few of the drivers I've coached over the years: Speedy, Flash, Stan Donit, Racer X, and Ace. As I said, the reason for introducing them to you and telling you their stories is for you to learn from their experiences. Are these real drivers and experiences? Yes and no. They are based on real coaching situations I've had, but the exact details have been changed "to protect the guilty."

What you will read below are excerpts of actual reports given to each driver before, during, or after the test session or race event. Again, my goal here is for you to recognize yourself—or at least part of yourself—in these drivers and learn from their experiences.

## Speedy: Re-programming Technique

Speedy is an excellent race driver. He's smart, consistent, and fast. He has been racing for more than 15 years. However, it seemed he had

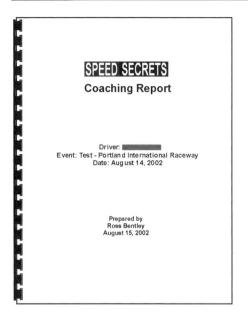

SPEED SECRETS

Coaching Report

Driver: ███████████
Event: Test - Portland International Raceway
Date: August 14, 2002

Prepared by
Ross Bentley
August 15, 2002

*This chapter consists of excerpts from some of the coaching reports I've written over the past few years for a variety of drivers.*

reached a plateau at one particular track—and especially one turn. He felt (and the data acquisition confirmed) he was a little slow in comparison to his competitors in this particular turn, and he was not making any progress. He had been driving this same turn at the same speed for the past few years, no matter how capable the car.

Speedy and I spent some time talking about his technique through this section of the track, and I came up with a plan for him that we both hoped would help him make progress. I was confident that if he did his homework, he would make some big gains.

Some of the things that he seemed to keep saying in our conversations were, "I just can't seem to go any faster there," and "I'm stuck at one speed through there—a slow speed." It was obvious to me that his belief system was part of the limiting factor. However, it would have done no good to simply tell him to change his beliefs. After all, they had been built on real experiences. So, to change his beliefs about his speed in this section of the track, we needed to change his experience, both physically and mentally. In other words, he first needed to physically drive that section of the track a little quicker, to prove to himself that he could do it. Even a very small gain would open his belief system up to further change. Then, he could reinforce and build from that with mental programming—before and after physically driving it.

It was also apparent he was trying too hard to go faster, and if you don't already know, I don't believe in trying. Trying is driving at the conscious level, and a person can only drive a race car well at the subconscious level.

My objectives were to begin to change his beliefs and do some re-programming of his physical techniques. In our conversation, we determined that his dominant or primary learning style was kinesthetic—he needed to feel or experience things before they really became learned (programmed). The following is the plan I developed and told him to follow.

### STEP #1: Ask Yourself Some Questions

• Is there any reason why you cannot go faster through, and exit out of, the chicane?

• Do you have a physical deficiency that won't allow you to go faster?

• Do you have a mental deficiency that won't allow you to go faster?

• Do you really want to go faster?

• Are you willing to do what it takes to go faster?

• Can you drive a race car consciously, or are you better off relying on your subconscious program to drive the car? Did you know that your conscious mind processes information at 2,000 bits of information per second; while your subconscious mind processes *four billion* bits per second?

Please take some time, Speedy, to really consider the answers to these questions. This step is very important.

### STEP #2: Physical programming

You explained that you use your left foot for a little brake just prior to turning into the right-hander in the second part of the chicane to help set the car to turn in. You also mentioned that you seem to over-slow the car doing this. That is not surprising. What do you use your left foot for mostly? The clutch, right? How many years have you been physically programming your left foot to slam the clutch pedal down? Your left foot is not in the habit of (does not have a program for) gently depressing a pedal. You need to change that and build a program so that your left foot is more sensitive and adaptable.

Over the next month, whenever you are driving an automatic transmission vehicle on the street (if necessary, go rent one for a month), brake with your left foot. Allow it to learn the sensitivity, the subtle nuances that your right foot has for braking; physically program it.

Every time you approach a corner, and this is important—especially right-hand corners, such as freeway on- and off-ramps—use your left foot to give the brake pedal a very gentle, very light squeeze (even if the corner does not require any braking). Make sure that you do this braking early—prior to turning in—and get back on the throttle early. Simulate the second part of the chicane as much as possible. And, while doing this, imagine you are there, driving through the chicane.

Again, what you are doing is building, and then reinforcing, a program for your left-foot braking.

## STEP #3: Mental Programming

Choose a room in your house where you can ensure some privacy—no phone calls! If you have a steering wheel around, get it.

Get comfortable sitting in a chair. Have your wife sit on the floor facing you with her legs stretched out in front of her, the bottoms of her feet resting against the balls of your feet. Her feet are the brake and gas pedals. (She might want to grab a magazine or book to read while you are doing this).

[Note: The use of the steering wheel and someone's feet for pedals is critical since his dominant learning style is kinesthetic]

Take some time—one to five minutes—to get yourself relaxed and in an Alpha state. Do this by closing your eyes, breathing deeply, and counting your breaths. Notice your heart rate slowing down. Once you feel you have gotten to an Alpha state, you are ready to begin mental programming. (If you need any other info on Alpha state, take a look at *Inner Speed Secrets*—the chapter on brain wave states.)

See, *feel*, and hear yourself driving down the back straight, your right foot flat to the floor (pressing on your wife's left foot). As you approach your braking point, your right foot comes off the throttle and squeezes the brakes (wife's right foot). Your left goes to the clutch (imaginary), you downshift, turn in (this is where the real steering wheel comes in—hold it in your hands). Your right foot comes off the brake pedal and back over to the throttle and begins to squeeze it down to balance the car, and then down all the way to the floor as you exit the first part of the chicane. As you approach the right-hand, second part of the chicane, your left foot comes over and squeezes the brake pedal like you have always done. Your left foot comes off the brakes while turning in, you begin to get back on the throttle, and you accelerate out of the chicane and onto the straightaway.

As you reach the middle of the straightaway, mentally fade out and back into the back straight again.

This time, do all the same things, except when you reach the second part of the chicane, brake with your left foot a little sooner—making sure you are back to throttle as you turn in—and *lighter*. Ask your wife to gently tell you how much pressure you applied—10 percent less, 20 percent less, or whatever she feels. Keep running through this section of the track until she says you are **consistently** braking about 40 to 50 percent lighter than you were the first time through.

Keep driving this section for another five laps. Notice how you feel doing it this way. It feels wonderful, awesome—it's easy, flowing. You notice the extra momentum, the extra speed you are carrying through the second part of the chicane—you're flying through here. What's that? You're hitting the rev limiter on the straight now! Wow, this feels great! And, it's easy. The car seems stuck to the track. That braking a little lighter and earlier actually makes the car seem absolutely glued to the track—it is so much better balanced through here.

As you drive through each lap, make note of what you feel: the pitching forward of the car under braking, the roll as you corner, the squat under acceleration, the vibration through the steering wheel and the brakes. Does the steering feel lighter or heavier as you progressively turn the wheel more? Do you feel the car bind up when you turn the steering wheel? Do you feel the tires grind against the track surface through the corner and run free as you straighten the steering? Notice the g-forces against your body, feel the heat from the car. . . .

After running about five laps, mentally drive down pit lane and come to a stop in your pit. As the crew checks over the car, someone plugs in the laptop and downloads the data. He slips the laptop through the side window and into your hands. You check the overlay of the past five laps with your previous best. Wow! Look at that! Just through the second part of the chicane, you've picked up almost 5 miles per hour. And the curve is so smooth! What a great feeling! This is so much fun!

The crew gives you the signal to fire the engine, you hand the laptop back, and out you go again. Five more laps. Just a gentle, light squeeze with the left foot before turning. . . .

You notice you are not trying, you are just relying on your subconscious program to do the driving. This is so much easier. As you approach the second part of the chicane, you think to yourself "momentum." Now you are really flying through here. After five laps you come in again and check the laptop. Faster again! The momentum is awesome! You mention to the crew that if you keep this up they are going to have to raise the top gear ratio or you will be running out of revs on the front straight.

You drive five of these five-lap stints, each time coming in the pits, checking the progress on the data acquisition.

Finally, you get out of the car. Damn! Do you have to get out? This is way too much fun! As you walk back to the paddock, someone asks you what your lap times were. You say you don't know, that you hadn't paid any attention to them, but that it sure felt great out there. Someone else mentions that you did a 1:06.9. You think, "That's a nice little reward for all the preparation I did before coming here. But my performance, the progress, the learning—that's the real reward."

A driver comes up to you and mentions that he had followed you through the chicane and that "you were flying!" Another driver mentions that "you've got a monster motor in that thing, because you just blew me away on the exit of the chicane." You smile and think, "If you only knew."

Slowly and gently come back mentally into the room, eventually opening your eyes. Thank your wife for her great "pedals."

Do this exercise at least twice a day. Do it on the plane on your way to the track (you will have to fake the pedals). Do it in the hotel room. Do it in the team trailer.

## STEP #4: At-Track, Sensory Input Sessions

In your first session on the track, make it a sensory input session—a kinesthetic one. Take the entire session on the track and focus only on what you can feel. Forget about what kind of lap times you are doing. This is probably the best way to warm up, and re-acclimate yourself to a track anyway. Plus, you will give better feedback to the team about the car—what it feels like, what it is telling you.

At the end of that session, sit down and write out all the things you felt: pitch, roll, vibrations, g-forces, pressures, bumps, everything.

On the second day in your first session, make it an auditory session. Make note of everything you can hear, and write it down. And on the final day, make it a visual session.

Your goal is to be more sensitive to these things than you have ever been before. The better the sensory data you input to your brain—and the better the quality—the better the output from you brain. Meaning, the better the quality of your psychomotor skills, the better your performance.

### STEP #5: Driving Subconsciously

In all the other track sessions, just relax and rely on, or trust, your mental programs to drive the car. Don't try. You were able to do that in your mental imagery sessions, so why not in the car? I guarantee that if you try less and just allow yourself to drive and have fun, you will be faster than ever before.

One final thought, Speedy. I have seen it over and over again: A driver seems to reach a plateau, where "no matter what, I can't seem to get any faster." One of two things then occur. Either the driver does nothing about it other than complain, and stays at that plateau; or, the driver makes some changes, sometimes stays at that plateau for a little bit longer, and then Bam!, makes a big improvement.

I suspect you are at that point where it seems you are not making any progress, but any second now you will make a big step. If you follow this plan, I'm sure it will happen very soon—without trying.

The result? After the first day of a three-day test, Speedy came to me and said that number one, he had had more fun in the car that day than he had in years; and, he had gone faster than ever before. At the end of the test, he claimed he had enjoyed driving more than he had since his first couple of seasons of racing. It was obvious that he had focused on allowing his subconscious to do the driving, letting his conscious mind observe and enjoy the ride.

Based on his other comments, I could tell Speedy's belief system had been cracked open, and he was once again able to see making further progress—getting faster and faster still.

One of the most interesting things is that I was able to do all of this coaching over the phone. It wasn't until after he had been on the track and driven faster than ever before that we actually talked face to face. This was one of my first, but not last, successful over-the-phone coaching sessions. In fact, I'm using this approach more and more all the time, as it is impossible for me to physically be at every track a driver needs me.

## Flash: Corner Entry Speed

Quite a few drivers I speak to recognize that they over-slow the car on the entry of some turns. Of course, that's the first step to going faster—being aware of the problem. But, how do you fix the problem? That was the situation Flash was in. Here is the plan I suggested for him.

First of all, Flash, over-slowing the car for a corner is not an uncommon problem—many drivers do it. And, the good news is that you've already handled the first step in fixing it—being aware of the problem. So, let's fix it.

Why do you think you over-slow the car, even though you know you can carry more speed into this corner? The reason is that you are programmed to do that. And, why are you programmed to do it? Because you have done it that way over and over again, probably hundreds of times, each time you entered that turn. You've practiced entering the turn at that speed, and you've become very good at doing it.

As I'm sure you know by now, simply going out on the track and trying to enter the turn faster is not going to help. You've probably tried that lots of times by now, and it didn't work.

What you need to do is change that mental program. How do you do that? Well, you could leave it to the same approach that caused the first program—physical programming, or practice. But, that's going to take a lot of seat time on its own, and that costs money and takes too much time. So, let's speed up that process by using mental programming as well.

Remember, Flash, that if you have a clear mental picture of what you are trying to achieve, and you are aware of what you are doing right now, your mind will find a way of making the two match. In other words, you will fix the problem naturally. This is the MI + A = G that we talked about. You already are aware of what you are doing now—you have a mental picture of the speed you are slowing down to on entry to the turn. The next step, then, is to develop a very clear mental picture of what speed you want to enter the turn at.

I would like you to sit in a comfortable chair in a room where you cannot be disrupted. Close your eyes, relax, and breathe deep and slow. Continue to relax for a few minutes. When you feel you are at that Alpha/Theta state we've spoken about before, begin to picture yourself entering Turn 2. Make note of the speed you are traveling, how fast things pass by you, the pitch of the engine and sound of the wind, and the vibrations through the steering wheel, seat, and pedals. See, feel, and hear yourself braking, downshifting, and entering the turn. As you turn in and the car begins to take a set in the corner, you notice the car has lots of grip. In fact, you can feel that you could carry another 3 or 4 miles per hour.

Mentally, go back to the turn entry again, this time carrying more speed. See, feel, and hear the car traveling 4 miles per hour faster—notice everything happening just that much faster. As you turn in, the car slides just a little and you make nice smooth corrections with the steering. The car feels great—it's still got good grip, you hear and feel the tires working. Notice the turn going by quickly, and you begin to accelerate just as early and hard as before. Actually, the car feels more balanced and stuck to the track than ever before.

Again, mentally go back and do it all over many times. The more times you do this, and the more realistic you make it by including all of your senses, the quicker you will have changed your corner entry program—the sooner you will be carrying more speed into the corner.

Remember, if you can't do it mentally, you will never be able to do it physically. Looking at it another way, do it mentally and it will be easy to do it physically. And once you've done it physically, it makes the mental program that much stronger.

The next time Flash went out for a test day he was consistently three-tenths of a second quicker in Turn 2 alone. He had spent about 15 minutes, twice a day, for two weeks working on changing his mental programming, and the results showed. He was ecstatic! He also began to believe he could make other big gains by working on his mental programming. He saw how easy and effective it was. This confidence led to more mental "homework," which led to further gains. It continued to snowball for Flash, until he was totally dominating his class. The victories and trophies were great, but it was his sense of self-satisfaction and inner confidence that was most rewarding.

## Stan Donit: Personal Performance

Stan Donit was a successful businessman in his late twenties who had some thoughts of making a career driving race cars. The first time I coached him, we spent most of the day working on improving his sensory input, and a few brain integration exercises. Without any changes to the car, he improved his best lap time by slightly over one second.

The next time I coached Stan Donit was another test day later in the year, and he expected the same kind of improvement. In fact, he expected to be within a tenth of a second of the track record. Unfortunately, his car was definitely not up to the task. There was no way the car was ever going to get close to the track record, no matter who was driving it. That didn't stop Stan Donit from trying, though. And that was the real problem—he tried.

This situation led to a discussion about performance. Afterwards, I wrote and sent Stan Donit the following summary of my coaching session:

> Stan, I thought you drove very well. Is there more time left in you? I bet there is—but not much. I bet you were within a tenth of a second of the best the car was capable of. That would have come from putting together a "perfect" lap—from a little more time in the car at this track.
>
> Remember, all you can do is get 100 percent out of the car—no more. If you get 100 percent out of the car, you should be happy with your performance. Like I said, you came about as close to that as possible. Your performance was great! There were times, though, where you didn't look smooth—you were **trying**. That's why I suggested focusing on how the car felt, rather than on your lap times. You definitely looked smoother then. Your lap times also improved a couple of tenths.
>
> Here's a story from my personal experience:
>
> Driving the BMWs this year has been a real learning experience for me. Over the past few years, whenever I've had another driver co-drive with me, I've usually been quicker than him. So, to hop in one of these BMWs at Sebring and Las Vegas and have my co-driver go quicker than me really hurt the old ego. What did I do? I tried to drive faster. What happened? I didn't go faster, I began making mistakes (I have a reputation as being a driver that doesn't make mistakes), and I wasn't having any fun. I even began to get down on myself.
>
> Then, a couple of weeks before the next race, I was going over some of my coaching notes and it hit me. It was time to take some of my own advice! For two weeks, I did everything I could to prepare: integration exercises a couple of times a day, mental imagery sessions, programming driving in the zone . . . I went to the race prepared, confident and ready to have fun.

All race weekend I acted as if I was the one in the team to chase. But most important, when I drove the car I completely ignored the lap times. I focused entirely on the act of driving at the limit, the execution. I focused on every detail of the track. I felt the car do things I never knew it did—my senses were so sharp. I said to myself, "forget the lap times, focus on performance—on the act of driving, not the result."

I bet you can guess what happened. In every session throughout the weekend, I was the quickest, even though I didn't pay any attention to it. To me, I was just excited about getting 100 percent out of the car and myself. Wow, was that fun! And, after having my co-driver hand the car over to me in second place, 25 seconds behind our team car, I passed it on the last lap to win the race. The funny thing is, even though I got the results I wanted (being fastest, and winning), all I could think about was how great my personal performance had been—focusing on the act, rather than the result. It also felt great to personally prove what I teach once again.

Of course, it's amazing what a little success can do for your confidence. The following race, I won again. But, I will admit that there were times during practice sessions when I started to think about my lap times again—the result. I really had to focus on the act of driving. Don't get me wrong. I do care about the result—very much so. But I know that by focusing on it, I reduce my chances of getting the result I want. It is one of the toughest and most satisfying challenges involved in race driving.

The moral of the story: You need to prepare for the Mid-Ohio race weekend now. You have some great "video" in your head, Stan. Use that to actualize. See the car working the way you want, carrying more speed into the turns than you were today, getting back on the throttle earlier, staying on the throttle until the very last fraction of a second. You know that you are fast—you've proven that to yourself and everyone else at the past two races. In fact, you may be happy to know that I talked to a number of people who commented on how fast you were in the past couple of races. You've got a lot of people scared! When you get back to Mid-Ohio next week, act as fast as you are. Let people know you're there to do business again.

And when you're in the car, focus on driving, not your lap times. Let the car slide around—let it dance. Enjoy the feeling of it on the edge. Just have fun! The result will look after itself.

Stan Donit's result at the next race was his best all season, a fifth. More importantly, his performance was awesome.

## Racer X: Learning to Drive An Oval Track

I was asked to coach Racer X, a relatively inexperienced driver, during his first time on an oval. In many ways, driving an oval is no different than driving a road course; and yet, in other ways, it is very different. The main difference is in a driver's mental approach to the task.

*Once behind the wheel, there is only one thing you can control—your performance. One of the keys to consistent performance is focusing on your performance—the act of driving—and not on the result. If at any time you find yourself focusing on the result, think about one specific driving technique, such as how quickly you are turning the steering wheel entering the next turn.*

Prior to Racer X's first oval test, we spent some time talking about goals and objectives for the test. Then we laid out a plan to achieve them.

The specific things you need to focus on when driving the oval are:
- If the car doesn't feel right, come in. The consequences of a mechanical or handling problem on an oval are huge.
- Momentum is everything. Look far ahead, and think "get there."
- A smooth throttle-brake-throttle transition is critical.
- Being on the throttle through the corner is critical, even if that means braking or easing off early before the turns, as the car will then "take a set" or be balanced, all the way through the corner.

• Slow hands on the steering wheel—a progressive turn-in to the corner, an arc through the turn.

• Un-winding the steering out of the turns. Turning the steering wheel is a bad thing to do to a race car—it's like applying the brakes—so unwind the steering and let the car run free at the exit of the corners.

• Car set up is everything on an oval—you cannot overdrive a bad-handling car on an oval and get away with it.

• Always inch up on the limit—don't take too big of a jump.

• Qualifying mode. Physically practice (program) getting up to speed immediately and turning in a great qualifying lap.

The key here is not the details of what the objectives were, but that we had set out very specific objectives for our testing session. Without these specific objectives—and without the both of us thoroughly discussing and understanding them—it is doubtful we would have accomplished any of them.

## Ace: Post-Race Debrief

Ace was a young driver I coached for most of a season in an open-wheel, spec series. He had awesome skills behind the wheel, but being young, he needed some fine-tuning in and out of the car.

The following is an overview of the things we worked on and things that needed further work after a race weekend.

You need to eat properly throughout race weekends, Ace! You wouldn't start a race without enough fuel in your car. Why race without fuel in your body?! I know you may not feel like eating, but you will need to get in the habit of doing it, so you might as well start getting used to it now.

Vision: The car will follow your eyes . . . where you look is where the car will go. So remember, if you look directly at the apex of a corner, you will probably turn directly towards it—it won't be a smooth arc towards it. At the turn-in point, you need to look toward the apex, but you need to have a mental picture of how you're going to get there, in an arc. You need to look with a "curved" view or focus.

Once you get so that you can drive the line through all the corners consistently and accurately, there are three basic ways of working on going faster: (1) getting on the power sooner, smoother and harder; (2) increasing your corner entry speed (without delaying when you get back on the power); (3) braking later. Remember, you will gain more with your foot on the throttle than you will with your foot on the brakes. Concentrate on the first two above. In fact, at this stage, you will gain more by working on the first one, getting on the power early, than with anything else. Concentrate on that this weekend—getting on the power early, smooth, and hard!

You're right, the objective of every session and race is to be the fastest and win. But what leads to being the fastest and winning? Not "trying" to be fast and win. By maximizing your performance, you will automatically be fast and win. Do everything you can to maximize your own performance: eat well, visualize, assume the proper seating position, plan what you are going to work on each session (pick the three most important areas to improve), don't think too much about the competition, get help from everyone around you (mechanics, family, or friends).

Be careful not to set limits. Don't think too much about what lap time you will be happy with prior to a session, because it may not be good enough, it may not be fast enough, it may not "drive" you. Don't ever be satisfied with a lap time—you can always find a way to go faster. Don't set limits on yourself.

Passing. You only need to get alongside your competitor and the corner is yours. If you go past him any farther, you are giving him an opportunity to re-pass you.

Sometimes you need to be patient with the car, particularly at the turn-in point—let the car "rotate" and point towards where you want it to go before getting on the power. The result of being patient is often a faster exit speed. Which is better? Being fast in the middle of the corner or at the exit of the corner? Being fast at the exit is going to pay off all the way along the straight.

Preparation is not just one thing, it's everything! Preparation is the difference between the winner and the losers. Again, preparation is everything you do to win. It is the main reason why Senna was as good as he was. If you think it was all natural talent, you're wrong. Read some of the books about him; about how much more time he spent analyzing the track and the car; how much more time he spent practicing, training; how fanatical he was about what he ate, how much sleep he got.

The closer you run to the wall or the edge of the track, the less it will hurt if you do hit it, and, the less likely it is you will hit it. Let the car run free, unwind the steering wheel out of the turns—use all the track—don't scrub speed at the exits of corners.

Don't accuse anyone of doing anything they didn't absolutely do for sure. Think about it a lot first before saying anything. Would you have done the same thing in the same situation? And even if you don't agree with something someone else did, there probably isn't much you can do about it now, so why bother saying anything at all? Ignore it and get on with your own racing.

What you do outside of the car is just as important as what you do in the car. Remember, a big part of your job as a race driver is as a motivator/team leader. You can have all the talent in the world, but if you don't have absolutely everyone around you pulling for you, and helping you, you will not make it in this sport. There was a driver who once kicked Ayrton Senna's butt in Formula 3. Anyone who knows anything will agree that he had as much, or more, natural talent as anyone—he was brilliant in the car. But he was not brilliant (an understatement) outside of the car (at his first Grand Prix, in Austria, he was asked on Austrian Television what it felt like to race against the great Austrian two-time World Champion, Niki Lauda. His reply was something along the lines of, "Who? I could care less. . ." ). The teams did not enjoy working with him, the media didn't like him, he was a bad sport, and a poor spokesman for any sponsor. And where is he today? Who knows?! (In fact, I don't think he did more than a half dozen F1 races). How you present yourself outside of the car will play a huge role in the rides you get in the future. How you act, react, and interact with all the people around you will determine how often you win. If your actions do not motivate— if they de-motivate—your team, sponsors, family, mechanics, engineers, sponsor-hunters, whoever—you will not get the competitive rides you need, you will lose rides, and you will lose the edge you require to win. Always remember, Ace, if you're not doing everything possible to win, some of your competition is and that is probably what it takes for them to beat you, even if you have more natural talent. If you are unsportsmanlike outside of the car, sponsors will not go near you. Neither will mechanics, team owners, or coaches.

Don't blame the car. If it is something you can fix, then do that. If not (and in a spec series, rarely can you do something about it), deal with it. Learn to adapt your driving to the car.

There will always be good sessions/races and bad sessions/races. The key is to minimize the bad ones. No matter who you are, you will not be fastest every session. The important thing is to not be upset and beat yourself up mentally, but to learn from that session, and come up with a plan to make yourself fastest next session. In other words, when you are quickest, great! When you are not, think about what you can learn from it; think of it as a learning session and how to improve for the next session.

There is a limit to how much you can think about or concentrate on while driving. When you're thinking about how to go quicker in the next session/race, and you should be all the time (even if you are already the fastest), pick two or three key areas (prioritize them) and plan how to address them. Be very specific. It's not good enough to say, "I'm going to turn in later for Turn 1." That's not specific enough. You need to plan how you are going to turn-in later for Turn 1, exactly where you're going to turn in, and then visualize and imagine what it will look and feel like. Then move on to the next priority.

There is no point focusing on a problem. What you need to do is focus on how to deal with a problem; the solution; and specifically, a strategy and plan of how to achieve the solution.

Oh, and don't forget, this is all about learning. Every time you go to the track, you learn something. Don't miss out on something really valuable. Pay attention to everything.

Racing is a lot harder work than it looks, isn't it?! And the driving is the easy part! But don't forget to have fun. Believe me, it beats doing absolutely anything else for a living. I will also bet that when you're having fun, you perform better and win.

If someone should spin in front of you, don't look at them. Look where you want to go, not where you don't want to go. You need to visualize this, a lot. It's the only way to practice, short of having people actually spin in front of you (which is a hard thing to find volunteers for!).

When out-braking someone, stay close to them. If you move too far to the inside of the track, they can't see you, plus, you give them a better angle on the corner. If you are close to the other car, you force your line on it. And again, if you do hit, the closer you are together, the less the impact.

Never be defensive about *any* critique, whether from me or anyone else. You can learn something from everyone—no matter how much bad information you have to filter through before getting to the useful stuff.

Plus, your attitude—at least your perceived attitude—is going to make a big impact on your success in your career. So, even if you don't agree with what someone is telling you, act as if you do, act as if you really appreciate the input, act as if you are really paying attention. Then, go away and think about why they suggest what they do. There is always a reason for their advice. It may not seem right to you now, but once you figure out why they suggest that, it may be very useful information.

Don't be afraid to assume responsibility for errors and/or crashes, even if they are not all your fault. You will gain great respect from others by doing this. In fact, you will gain the most respect when taking the blame in cases where it is more clearly someone else's fault. You did this a bit when you crashed, and the team appreciated your attitude—even though they knew it was partially the other guy's fault. If you had put all the blame on the other guy, the team would have gotten defensive and blamed you even more. You would have taken the focus off of the other guy, and put it on you. Strange, isn't it?

You are the fastest driver. You are the best in the series. So be the best outside of the car as well. Be friendly, happy, enthusiastic, appreciative, and modest. Be confident, but not cocky.

If there is an opportunity to prove you are the best, prove it—even outside of the car. Sit at the front in drivers' meetings. Let everyone know where you intend to stay.

No matter what lap time you turn, you can always go faster. Don't *try* to go faster, but let yourself go faster—be smooth, and let the car flow. But don't be satisfied with any lap time. You need to go faster.

Again, the reason I present these coaching examples here is to get you thinking. Don't be afraid to read through them more than once. Often times, when you go back you will begin to recognize that you do some of the same things these drivers have done. One of the traits of a champion is learning from others' mistakes. Take advantage of some of my "students."

I hope you take something else away from these examples: The idea of writing down your own personal objectives and action plans for each and every session on the track. That's a big part of self-coaching yourself to a higher level of performance.

# Chapter 14

# *Superstar Theory*

Throughout this book, I've talked about, and used as examples, a number of great race drivers, especially Michael Schumacher. Am I the president and founder of the Michael Schumacher fan club? No, but at the time of writing this book, he is generally recognized as the best in the world, and one of the best of all time, so who better to use as a role model for comparison? Do I think he is something special? Yes and no.

I believe all of us—you, me, Michael Schumacher—were born with the same amount of natural driving talent. We all have the ability to be a superstar. Yes, if you were born with DNA that caused you to be 6 feet, 10 inches, it is doubtful you are going to make a career out of driving F1 cars. But, assuming you have the basic physical design, you too can be a racing superstar. In other words, Schumacher was not born special.

If there is a difference between Michael Schumacher and you today, it is simply a result of what the two of you have done with the talent with which you were born. And yes, that makes him special.

The bottom line is this: There were a number of events in Schumacher's life that enabled him to take the basic talent he was born with and turn that into the superstar abilities he demonstrates today.

If you read *Inner Speed Secrets*, you know the value of being integrated (whole-brained) to achieving peak performance. That is, using both halves of your brain equally—the creative, intuitive, and big-picture right hemisphere and the factual, logical, and detail-oriented left hemisphere. Whereas many children do not do enough physical movement as a baby to become as integrated as possible, I suspect Schumacher did. When a small child does become integrated, he or she feels and acts more coordinated. That leads to a belief system that tells him he's coordinated, which encourages more physical movement. This belief system is reinforced by comments from outside sources (parents, friends, teachers). All of this encourages the child to do more physical movement that further enhances brain integration and so on. It becomes a self-fulfilling prophecy.

Of course, the opposite is true, as well. For example, a baby that does not do much "cross crawling" action may not become as integrated as early in life, which affects the belief system. This leads to a child who stays away from physical activities "because I'm not very good at it."

So, Schumacher enters childhood at an integrated, coordinated level. I'm sure that encouraged him to participate in numerous sports, which led to the development of his sensory input skills. The fact that his family had its own karting track certainly didn't hurt. But, from what I understand about his childhood, he didn't simply spend a lot of time in a kart—he spent a lot of well-defined time in a kart. In other words, he went onto the kart track with specific strategies for improving.

You see, much of the development of his natural talent was a result of the environment in which he grew up.

Now, I'm not suggesting that Schumacher necessarily developed these abilities at a conscious level. Actually, I'm guessing he stumbled into most of the techniques, just like many people who become good at a physical task. On top of that, I suspect some techniques were taught to him, in a very specific manner.

One of the things that separate Schumacher—or any other superstar— from the rest is his ability to learn so very quickly—more quickly than most everyone else. Assuming he started his racing career with the same talent level as everyone around him, he was able to take that talent and develop it and enhance it faster. That is what gives him the edge.

Of course, that does not come from wishful thinking, nor without some effort. He is famous for the amount of time he spends working out physically. I know a similar effort goes into his mental preparation. I know that was also the case with Ayrton Senna. After a full day of testing, where he has completed the equal of two full race distances, Schumacher is often seen lifting weights and training. At that point, you have to ask, is that natural talent or hard work that got him to where he is today?

My main point is this: It doesn't matter how much natural talent you believe you were born with, it is what you do with it. If you learn how to learn to be better faster than other people with similar talent, you will be miles ahead.

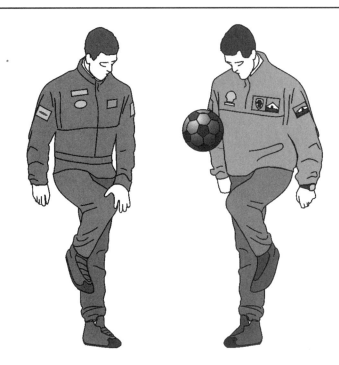

*Many drivers have asked whether Michael Schumacher does brain integration exercises. I don't know if he does specific exercises, such as cross crawls, but I do know he does warm-up by practicing with a soccer ball—which is very similar to cross crawls, and would have the same effect.*

### SPEED SECRET #33:
### *Learn how to learn and you will never stop improving.*

Of course, that is my intention as well—to continue to learn more about the art, science, traits, and techniques that lead drivers to become champions. So, rather than saying, "until we meet again" I will say, "until I learn more . . . "

Be quick, and as I remind every driver I coach prior to a race, "have fun!"

# *More Speed Secrets*

1. No matter what level of racing you participate in, you are a team builder.
2. Surround yourself with the right people and your career will look after itself.
3. Marketing skills are every bit as important to your career as driving fast.
4. Adapt and improvise to become a master race driver.
5. Have fun!
6. If you believe you can't, you can't. If you believe you can, you can.
7. The more complete a package you are, the more successful you will be.
8. MI + A = G.
9. Increase your awareness by debriefing—even with yourself.
10. If it seems you are not improving, you are about to.
11. Drive in your mind before driving on the track.
12. Delete your expectations. Focus on your possibilities.
13. The more quantity, and the higher the quality of sensory information going into your brain, the better the quality the output will be—the better you will drive.
14. Practice—everyday—being aware.
15. Use your street driving to make you a better track driver.
16. Regularly use traction sensing sessions to improve your ability to drive at the limit.
17. Drive the car at the very limit for every segment, for every turn, for every lap.
18. The faster the corner, the closer to the geometric line you should drive; the slower the corner, the more you need to alter your line with a later apex.
19. Focus on the most important corner first—and the least important last.

20. You can only use 100 percent of the tires' traction—and make sure you do.
21. Every inch of track you are not using is costing you speed. You paid for it, so use it all.
22. Corner entry speed is more important than late braking.
23. The faster and longer the corner, the less trail braking you should use and the earlier you need to be on the power; the slower and tighter the corner, the more trail braking you should use to help rotate the car.
24. The slower the corner, the later the apex, the quicker and crisper you need to turn the steering wheel; the faster the corner, the more you need to arc or bend the car into the turn with slow hands.
25. The less change in speed through a corner, the faster you will be.
26. Fast mid-corner speed comes from great entry speed, car balance, and early exit speed.
27. Sensory input and awareness are the keys to driving fast—no matter how the corners appear.
28. Improve your adaptability through knowledge and practice.
29. The higher a car's moment of inertia, the earlier and more gently you need to turn in.
30. The more reference points you have, the fewer errors you will appear to make.
31. Minimize errors through maximizing sensory input.
32. Just because a change doesn't work the first time, re-think and try it again. Alter your technique to make the increase in speed work.
33. Learn how to learn and you will never stop improving.

# Self-Coaching Questions

- How far ahead do I look when driving on the highway? How about when driving on city streets? On the racetrack? Can I look farther ahead?

- How consistent is my corner entry speed? Does my speed at the turn-in point vary from lap to lap by 1 mile per hour? Three miles per hour? Five or more miles per hour?

- When was the last time I worked on developing—on practicing—my traction sensing skills? When was the last time I practiced just sliding a car around, whether on a skid pad or the racetrack?

- How tightly do I grip the steering wheel when driving on the street? How about when driving on the racetrack? Can I relax my grip a bit?

- Where am I in the continuous learning process loop? Have I perfected the line? How about the exit phase? How is my corner entry? My mid-corner speed?

- What can I do to improve my line? My corner exit? My corner entry? Mid-corner? Turn in later or earlier? More gently or crisper? Begin accelerating earlier, or just get on the throttle harder at the same place? Carry more speed into the corner, or slow it down 1 mile per hour or so to get the car to turn in better? Make a smoother transition from brake to throttle? Turn the steering wheel less, or begin unwinding it out of the turn earlier?

- What would happen if I turned in 1 or 2 feet later? Earlier? Would I have to change my corner entry speed to do that? Exactly where would my turn-in reference point be then?

- Am I apexing too early? Too late? Is the car at the right angle when I pass the apex—pointing in the direction I want at that point?

- Am I unwinding the steering from the apex on out? Am I "releasing" the car from the corner, letting it "run free" at the exit?

- Which is the most important corner on the track from a lap time/speed point of view? Which is second most important? Third, and so on?

• At which corner do most drivers have the most difficulty? At which corner can I gain the biggest advantage over my competition?

• In working on the car's setup, which corner should I focus on first?

• Am I using all of the tires' traction when accelerating out of the corners?

• What would happen if I started accelerating sooner? If I squeezed on the throttle quicker? Am I causing the car to understeer or oversteer by accelerating too abruptly or hard? Can I squeeze on the throttle smoother?

• Am I holding the car in the corner too long? Can I unwind the steering sooner?

• Before I get to the apex, am I looking for and through the exit point and down the straightaway?

• Can I carry 1 mile per hour more into the corner? Two mile per hour? Three mile per hour? What will happen if I carry more speed into the corner? Will I still be able to make the car turn in and "rotate" towards the apex? Will it delay when I begin accelerating?

• Can I left-foot brake in my car? Do I have the sensitivity with my left foot to do so? Does my left foot have the necessary programming?

• Am I "snapping" my foot off the brake pedal—coming off too quickly? Can I ease off the pedal more gently? How would that feel if I did? Just how gently can I come off the brake?

• Am I easing off the brake pedal too slowly, thereby trail-braking too long? Is that causing the car to rotate too quickly, to oversteer during the entry?

• Am I turning the steering wheel too quickly or too slowly? Does the car respond to my initial turn of the wheel? What if I turned the wheel more quickly or slowly? Can I be smoother with the wheel? What would it feel like if I turned the wheel more smoothly? More slowly? More quickly? Do I have slow hands or quick hands?

- Am I over-slowing the car on entry? Is that resulting in me getting on the throttle too hard, causing "change-in-speed oversteer?" What do I need to do to make the car turn in with more speed? Do I need to trail brake more or less? Do I need to change my line slightly—turn in earlier or later? Do I need to turn the steering wheel more crisply, or slowly and progressively?

- Am I blipping the throttle enough to ensure a smooth downshift? At the right time? Am I blipping it too much, causing the car to lurch forward?

- How's the car's balance during the entry phase of the corner? How about in the mid-corner phase? What can I do to improve the car's balance? Ease off the brakes more gently? Be more progressive with the steering input? Squeeze on the throttle more smoothly? Make a smoother transition from braking to throttle?

**About the author:**

Ross Bentley lives and breathes racing and has done so since the age of five. In addition to driving just about everything in is 25 years (and counting) of racing cars, he has developed a great understanding and knowledge of practically all aspects of a career in motorsport: team management; race car engineering; mechanics and fabrication; marketing and sponsorship; public relations; and career building. In other words, he knows what makes the complete driver.

Ross has made a career driving race cars and coaching race drivers. The list of cars he has raced and won in includes sprint cars, Formula Ford, Trans-Am, Showroom Stock, GT, Prototype Sports Cars and Indy cars. The drivers he has coached have raced and won in everything from entry-level, spec series, open-wheel cars to CART Champcars, and from autocrossing to NASCAR.

Ross's long-term goals are to develop race drivers and non-race drivers into complete race drivers. Through his Speed Secrets Driver Development Services, and in his role as driver development director for Quantum Autosports, he's committed to helping create the racing champions of the future.

For more information on Ross's driver development services, go to www.speed-secrets.com. He can be reached at info@speed-secrets.com for questions or comments.

# Index

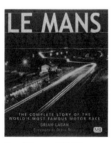